Air Band Radio Handbook

Air Band Radio Handbook

David J. Smith

PSL

PATRICK STEPHENS
Wellingborough, Northamptonshire

First published in 1986
Second edition 1987

British Library Cataloguing in Publication Data

Smith, David J.
Air band radio handbook.—2nd ed.
1. Air traffic control—Great Britain
I. Title
629.136′6′0941 TL725.3.T7

ISBN 1-85260-047-0

Patrick Stephens Limited is part of the Thorsons Publishing Group

Reproduced, printed and bound in Great Britain by
Hazell Watson & Viney Limited,
Member of the BPCC Group,
Aylesbury, Bucks

2 4 6 8 10 9 7 5 3

Contents

Introduction

Prior to 1963 enthusiasts had to rely on their own eyesight, aided by binoculars and telescopes, to identify aircraft. A minor revolution occurred in that year when the first radios covering the VHF air band (110–136 mhz) were put on the market. The messages between pilots and ground controllers could now be overheard by anyone who cared to buy one. More important, the majority of aircraft flying over could be identified by their registration or serial number.

These early sets were neither cheap nor very portable but over the years the trend towards miniaturisation has brought us pocket-sized sets from many manufacturers. Also, if one is prepared to part with several hundred pounds, there are magnificent receivers which scan the entire band automatically, or can be pre-set to receive only those local frequencies which may be of interest.

A great many people have bought air band radios, however, and found the jargon they hear almost incomprehensible. It is easy to pick out callsigns but most VHF listeners I have talked to would like to build up a better picture of what is going on and to unravel the 'mysteries' of Air Traffic Control. This book aims to do just that.

Similarly, people embarking upon a course of flying lessons for a Private Pilot's Licence would find it useful to acquire an air band radio and listen to how the professionals do their R/T. My experience shows that to the majority of trainee pilots learning how to use the radio is almost as big a hurdle as mastering their aircraft. Nothing brands one as an amateur so much as the long, rambling transmissions which controllers have to face on numberless occasions on a busy frequency! Some people may have been flying for years with a lot of skill but they let themselves down by poor R/T technique.

The terse messages, so confusing at first hearing, follow a definite pattern known as 'standard phraseology'. This verbal shorthand is designed to impart the maximum amount of unambiguous information in the shortest possible time. Since English is the international language of Air Traffic Control it must be understood easily by those with a different native tongue. With careful listening, and the aid of the examples in this book, the R/T exchanges on the air band will soon become both logical and familiar.

It must be emphasised that in the extremely complex world of Air Traffic Control procedures are changing all the time; new air lanes may be brought into use, others replaced or re-routed. Similarly new beacons and reporting points are always being introduced. Frequencies tend to stay the same for years, although with the current introduction of closer spacing between them there may be some upheavals in the future. The fact that radio navigation charts are updated every month or so shows just how frequently changes are liable to occur.

Acknowledgements

My grateful thanks to the Civil Aviation Authority, IAL Aviation Services, Fairbotham & Co Ltd, Dave Mobbs, Margaret and Adrian Thompson and Ken Rodgers for their help in the preparation of this book.

Abbreviations and Q-Codes

ADF	Automatic Direction Finder
ADR	Advisory Route
ADT	Approved Departure Time
AFIS	Aerodrome Flight Information Service
AGL	Above Ground Level
AIS	Aeronautical Information Service
ATCC	Air Traffic Control Centre
ATD	Actual Time of Departure
ATIS	Automatic Terminal Information Service
BAA	British Airports Authority
CAA	Civil Aviation Authority
CAAFU	Civil Aviation Authority Flying Unit
CHAPI	Compact Helicopter Approach Path Indicator
D/F	Direction Finding
DFR	Departure Flow Regulation
DFTI	Distance From Touchdown Indicator
DME	Distance Measuring Equipment
EAT	Expected Approach Time
ETA	Estimated Time of Arrival
ETD	Estimated Time of Departure
FIR	Flight Information Region
GMC	Ground Movement Control
GMP	Ground Movement Planning
GPWS	Ground Proximity Warning System
HF	High Frequency
ICAO	International Civil Aviation Organisation
IFR	Instrument Flight Rules
ILS	Instrument Landing System
IMC	Instrument Meteorological Conditions
INS	Inertial Navigation System
IRVR	Instrumented Runway Visual Range
LATCC	London Air Traffic Control Centre
LITAS	Low Intensity Two Colour Approach Slope Indicators

MATZ	Military Aerodrome Traffic Zone
MDH	Minimum Descent Height
MLS	Microwave Landing System
MOR	Mandatory Occurrence Report
NDB	Non-Directional Beacon
OCH	Obstacle Clearance Height
PAPIS	Precision Approach Path Indicator System
PAR	Precision Approach Radar
PPR	Prior Permission Required
QDM	Magnetic track to the airfield with nil wind
QFE	Barometric pressure setting at aerodrome level
QGH	Controlled descent through cloud
QNH	Barometric pressure at sea level
QTE	True bearing from the airfield
RAS	Radar Advisory Service
RIS	Radar Information Service
RIV	Rapid Intervention Vehicle
R/T	Radio Telephony
RVR	Runway Visual Range
SAR	Search and Rescue
SID	Standard Instrument Departure
SRA	Surveillance Radar Approach
SRZ	Special Rules Zone
SSR	Secondary Surveillance Radar
STAR	Standard (Instrument) Arrival Route
TAF	Terminal Aerodrome Forecast
TMA	Terminal Control Area (formerly Terminal Manoeuvring Area)
UHF	Ultra High Frequency
UTC	Universal Co-ordinated Time
VASI	Visual Approach Slope Indicator
VDF	VHF Direction Finder
VHF	Very High Frequency
VMC	Visual Meteorological Conditions
VOR	VHF Omni-Directional Range

Chapter 1

Listening

What you can hear, and in turn relate to aircraft you see flying overhead, obviously depends on the position of your location relative to airports and air lanes. Since VHF radio waves follow approximate lines of sight, the higher the aircraft, the farther away you can hear messages from it. Transmitter power is also a factor but, generally speaking, high flying aircraft can be received up to 200 miles away. As a rule of thumb, frequencies below 123 mhz are allocated to tower and approach units and those above 123 mhz to Air Traffic Control Centres (ATCCs), although there are exceptions to this.

Ground stations may be screened by hills, buildings and other obstructions, so you may not be able to pick up the replies from a tower or approach unit if you live more than ten miles away from it. The coverage for the ATCCs at London and Prestwick and the Sub-Centre at Manchester is very much better, however, there being few places in the flatter parts of the British Isles out of range of one or more of the powerful transmitters. This is because they are sited at some distance from their associated ground stations, usually on high ground. There may, however, be some 'blind spots' in reception for no apparent reason.

The first thing to do is to establish which ground stations are within range and which can help you to identify aircraft flying in your local area. If you are fortunate enough to own a scanning receiver you can set up the appropriate frequencies and monitor them when required. With experience you will soon know which station an aircraft is likely to be 'working', its height being a good clue as to whether it is talking to the local airfield, ATCC, radar unit etc. Unfortunately in an area such as the Midlands there are so many ATC units capable of giving a radar service that it may be difficult to discover to which a transit aircraft is talking. A flight below airways in the South Midlands, for example, might be in contact with Upper Heyford, Bedford or Brize

Norton Radar units or simply the London Flight Information frequency. Of course, the pilot might not be talking to anyone, nor does he need to if he keeps clear of aerodrome traffic zones and other restricted airspace.

If you have the good fortune to live beneath an airway and, even better, close to one of its reporting points, the relevant airways frequency can be selected and you can sit back and wait for something interesting to appear. Alas, rare aircraft seem to have a tendency to fly over when there is a solid cloud layer and only a tantalising drone or rumble can be heard! Unfortunately, it is not just a simple case of listening in, running outside at the right moment and rapidly filling up one's notebooks. Aircraft do not always use their registrations or serial numbers as callsigns, the trend in commercial flying is for more and more companies to use a callsign totally unrelated to what is painted on the aircraft. The airlines have been doing this for years but the practice has now spread even to taxi aircraft.

The answers to any questions which may arise from this practise, for the most part, are to be found in the network of enthusiasts' magazines which keep most airfields under surveillance and publish detailed lists of visitors, usually tabulated by callsign as well as registration letters. The information is normally acquired by courtesy of the airport management or ATC, the ranks of which are riddled with enthusiast 'moles'. Some private airfields, such as those run by British Aerospace, which operate military aircraft are understandably less co-operative, but there is often a local spotter who makes notes and passes them on! Since most transatlantic flights from north-west Europe have to cross Britain at some point even those anonymous airliners on contrails can be identified as there are several publications available which match the callsign and registration of most of them.

Identifying military aircraft is very difficult as few use the actual serial number, USAF transports being one of the few exceptions. Military airfields generally use UHF frequencies to talk to their own aircraft, which is outside the scope of this book. However, UHF receivers, hitherto virtually unobtainable, are now on the market, but little can be learned from the R/T about the aircraft involved.

Bearing in mind that air traffic has its rush hours too, certain times of the day can be particularly rewarding for air band listeners. For example, the Heathrow peak period for arriving traffic is mid-morning, reflected in the increased landing fees at this time. Late afternoon, particularly on Fridays, sees an even larger volume of traffic in the congested United Kingdom airways system as the entire

British executive fleet seems intent upon making for home!

For insomniacs there is plenty going on even in the smallest hours of the night as aircraft flying the mail wend their way towards Liverpool and East Midlands five nights a week from all points of the compass and fan out again some time later. Heathrow has a virtual ban on traffic after midnight because of noise restrictions, but Luton, Manchester, Glasgow and others send load after load of holiday-makers to the Mediterranean and beyond, particularly on summer weekends. Mixed in are the cargo aircraft, most of them scheduled, but occasionally including an extra service rushing some urgently needed parts for the motor industry.

Finally, a note about the law relating to air band listening. In a word, it is illegal for the unlicensed! However, if the listener does not impart the information he hears to another person it would seem to be permissible. Judging by the number of radios one hears blasting out across public viewing areas at airports, it would appear that officialdom turns a blind eye to what is essentially a harmless activity. The law may be changed one day but in the meantime do not telephone the newspapers if you overhear a hijack or some other emergency in progress. This sort of thing could end the authorities' tacit acceptance of air band listening.

In 1965 there was some trouble caused by cheap super-regenerative receivers which actually re-transmitted the received signal. The resulting carrier wave interfered with air to ground communications and air band radios were banned on Manchester Airport's public viewing galleries, unless the owner had a dispensation from the telecommunications section which offered a free testing service. This seems to have been the only time when air band radios have ever been controlled in this country and there is no evidence that it was done at any other British airport.

Right *The new 45 m high Control Tower at Gatwick* (CAA).

DAN-AIR LONDON

Chapter 2

ATC terminology

The majority of air band listeners use their radio as a means of logging aircraft registrations but there are others for whom this is of no more than academic interest. Their listening pleasure is derived from learning how aircraft are controlled and the way the ATC system operates. Those in the second category will soon begin to grasp the principles, and will want to find out more, whilst those in the first will recognise that a basic knowledge of them will assist in tracking the aircraft in which they are interested.

Before I embark upon a more detailed description of ATC I should like first to cast some light on the jargon words which seem to puzzle the new air band listener. The most obvious are the terms QNH, QFE and Flight Level. The first two are codes rather than abbreviations and refer to the current atmospheric pressure at sea level and aerodrome level respectively. When the value in millibars is set on the aircraft's altimeter the instrument will indicate the distance above the appropriate datum. The term QFE Threshold refers, by the way, to the barometric pressure converted to that at the end of a runway.

Above a point known as the transition altitude, normally between 3,000 ft and 6,000 ft in the United Kingdom, a standard setting of 1013.2 millibars is used, producing what is termed a Flight Level (abbreviated to FL). This ensures that all aircraft, particularly within controlled airspace, are flying on the same altimeter setting and can thus easily be separated vertically by the required amount. This obviates the necessity of continually adjusting the altimeter to allow for local pressure variations over the route, any error being common to all aircraft in the system. FL 70 is roughly equivalent to 7,000 ft, FL 230 to 23,000 ft and so on.

Times are given in the form of two figures; for example 14, pronouced one-four, indicates 14 minutes past the hour, four-two 42 minutes past the hour and so on. The standard ATC time in the United

Kingdom, and indeed in the entire aviation world, is Universal Co-ordinated Time, known as UTC (sic). In the winter it is the same as local or *Alfa* time in the United Kingdom but during the British Summer Time period it is one hour behind. This use of UTC ensures that there is no confusion with Flight Plans on aircraft transitting time zones.

The word *squawk* is often heard, particularly in route clearances, along with a four figure code. This is set on the aircraft's transponder, a device which responds to automatic interrogations from a ground station by sending a return signal in coded form. The information appears on the radar screen as a label giving callsign, height and destination, adjacent to the appropriate aircraft position symbol. (The word *blip* is now somewhat outmoded, the image on the screen on modern airways radars being produced electronically via a computer. The centre sweep familiar in films is now only seen on approach radars at the smaller airports.)

The term *clearance* or *cleared* is a legal one meaning that the aircraft may proceed under certain explicit conditions and that it will not be impeded by other traffic. It has, in the past, been somewhat over-used by controllers in circumstances where its use was unnecessary so the authorities have narrowed it down considerably. It is now confined mainly to route clearances and runway occupancy for take-off and landing, thus avoiding any possible confusion with the meaning.

Directions are given in degrees magnetic so that if an aircraft is heading 360° it is flying due north, 090° due east and so on. Note the difference between heading and actual path over the ground (track). If there is a strong cross-wind an aircraft may be pointing (heading) in a particular direction but travelling over the ground in a considerably different direction. There is an analogy here with rowing a small boat across a fast-flowing river, although you may be aiming for a point on the opposite bank, the current will also be deflecting you sideways. Simple right and left are used for direction changes, as in the instruction 'Turn right heading 340', port and starboard being long outmoded in aviation.

Speed is expressed in knots, one knot being equal to one nautical mile per hour. The exception to this is on transatlantic and similar long-haul flights where a Mach Number is employed, speed being expressed as a ratio of the speed of sound. Jet transports cruise at around Mach 0.8 and Concorde at Mach 2, twice the speed of sound.

Distances are measured in nautical miles (approx 2,025 yd). References to DME, as in 'Report 8 DME Wallasey', relate to the

Distance Measuring Equipment carried aboard aircraft. This receives radio transmissions from ground beacons and enables the distance to or from the particular position to be presented automatically to the pilot as a continuous read-out in miles and tenths. In some systems, the 'time to go' to the beacon can also be displayed to the pilot.

Runways are designated by two numbers derived from the heading in degrees magnetic. The main runway at Manchester, for example, is 06/24. This is rounded up from the actual direction of 057/237° magnetic and the end zero omitted. Similarly a heading of 054/234 would be presented as 05/23. Other familiar examples are 10 Right/28 Left and 10 Left/28 Right at Heathrow and 08/26 at Gatwick.

Somewhat confusing to the layman are the terms VFR, IFR, VMC and IMC, so I shall explain them at some length because they are of paramount importance in ATC. Flight conditions are divided thus:

(a) Visual Flight Rules (VFR) which apply under Visual Meteorological Conditions (VMC);

(b) Instrument Flight Rules (IFR) which apply under Instrument Meteorological Conditions (IMC).

VFR applies to flights between 3,000 ft and 25,000 ft outside controlled airspace only when the pilot has good visibility ('good' being defined as a minimum of five miles) and is able to remain at least one mile horizontally and 1,000 ft vertically clear of cloud. At or below 3,000 ft above mean sea level in uncontrolled airspace, an aircraft flying at an indicated airspeed (IAS) of 140 kt or less must remain in sight of the ground or water and clear of cloud in a flight visibility of at least one mile. If the IAS is more than 140 kt, the flight visibility must be at least three miles and the aircraft must keep at least one mile horizontally and 1,000 ft vertically from cloud. (Here springs to mind the story of the pilot who said 'Oh yes, we've got three miles, one in front and one out each side!')

Since it is his or her responsibility to keep clear of other traffic, the pilot must maintain a good look-out. Furthermore, under certain conditions, climbs or descents maintaining VMC may be authorised for aircraft flying under IFR so as to expedite traffic, it is then the pilot's responsibility to avoid other traffic. In R/T transmissions the terms VFR or Victor Fox are used freely. Similarly, VMC may be referred to as Victor Mike. The phrase 'VMC on top' means that the aircraft is flying in VMC conditions above a cloud layer.

IFR comes into force when the visibility requirements described above cannot be met, and at all times during the hours of darkness. It is then mandatory for aircraft to be flown on instruments by a suitably qualified pilot. It must also carry a minimum scale of navigational and other equipment. Within controlled airspace, responsibility for separation from other aircraft is in the hands of ground controllers.

Outside controlled airspace, pilots flying above the transition altitude of 3,000 ft must reset their altimeters to the standard setting of 1,013 millibars and fly in accordance with what is known as the quadrantal rule. This is intended to ensure that aircraft on converging headings at levels below 24,500 ft remain clear of each other by at least 500 ft, as the following table explains:

Magnetic track	*Cruising level*
Less than 90°	Odd thousands of feet
90° but less than 180°	Odd thousands of feet plus 500 ft
180° but less than 270°	Even thousands of feet
270° but less than 360°	Even thousands of feet plus 500 ft

Above 24, 500 ft the semi-circular rule applies:

Magnetic track	*Cruising level*
Less than 180°	25,000 ft
	27,000 ft
	29,000 ft or higher levels at intervals of 4,000 ft
180° but less than 360°	26,000 ft
	28,000 ft
	31,000 ft or higher levels at intervals of 4,000 ft

A final variation on the IFR/VFR theme is Special VFR, an authorisation by ATC for a pilot to fly within a control zone, even though he is unable to comply with IFR and in certain special rules airspace where provision is made for such flights. The minimum weather conditions which limit these clearances vary at different locations. VFR flight is allowed in Special Rules Zones but when the visibility falls to 9 km or below, and/or the cloud ceiling drops to less than 1,500 ft, a Special VFR clearance is issued.

Standard separation is provided between all Special VFR flights, and between such flights and other aircraft operating IFR. In practice much use is made of geographical features to keep Special VFR traffic apart, routeing along opposite banks of an estuary for instance. When flying on this type of clearance a pilot must comply with ATC instructions and remain at all times in flight conditions which enable him to determine his flight path and to keep clear of obstructions. It is implicit in all Special VFR clearances that the aircraft stays clear of cloud and in sight of the surface. ATC almost always imposes a height limitation which will require the pilot to fly either at or below a specific level. A typical clearance at Liverpool, for example, is 'GYE is cleared to the zone boundary via Chester, Special VFR not above 1,500 ft Liverpool QNH 1002.'

The phrase 'Rule 21 Airspace' is heard from time-to-time on R/T; it simply means that in certain airspace such as airways and Control Zones IFR applies all the time, regardless of actual weather conditions. It refers to the Rules of the Air and Air Traffic Control contained in the UK Air Navigation Order.

Phonetic alphabet

The use of phonetics on radio to overcome the problems of confusing similar sounding letters like 'B' and 'P' or 'M' and 'N' dates back to the First World War when it was essential that such information as map references were passed accurately by aircraft spotting for the artillery. The phonetic alphabet of the time began A-Ack, B-Beer and has left us with such enduring phrases as 'Ack-Ack' for anti-aircraft fire. I am not certain when this alphabet was superseded but by the time of the Second World War it was as follows:

A — Able	J — Jig	S — Sugar
B — Baker	K — King	T — Tare
C — Charlie	L — Love	U — Uncle
D — Dog	M — Mike	V — Victor
E — Easy	N — Nan	W — William
F — Fox	O — Oboe	X — X-Ray
G — George	P — Peter	Y — Yoke
H — How	Q — Queen	Z — Zebra
I — Item	R — Roger	

In the fifties, by international agreement, the British wartime code was replaced by a new alphabet designed to be more easily pronounced by aircrew whose native language was other than English. Some of the original phonetics were retained but a number of words known throughout the world were now employed. The resulting alphabet was almost identical to that in use today, the exceptions being M — Metro, N — Nectar and X — Extra.

The new offering sparked off some ribald comment that its originators seemed to have spent a lot of time hanging around in bars and dancehalls, such was the emphasis on these admirable pursuits! The alphabet was overhauled once more in 1956 and remains in use to this day. My only subjective criticism is that Juliet and Zulu can be confused, admittedly not very often, when used by certain foreign nationals against a background of engine noise. Papa is another weak point. Correctly it should be pronounced Pah-*Pah* but this is more difficult to say and most pilots and controllers pronounce it with equal emphasis on the two syllables.

Certain universally accepted codes and abbreviations, such as QNH, QFE, ILS, SRA, QDM are not put into phonetics but said as written. There is also a standard way of pronouncing numbers and the word decimal, as used in radio frequencies, is supposed to be said as 'dayseemal' although this rarely happens in practice. (I once heard an Irish pilot who, after the controller used the word 'tree' to him for three, accused him of 'takin' da micky'!)

Current phonetic alphabet

A —Alfa	J —Juliet	S —Sierra
B —Bravo	K —Kilo	T —Tango
C —Charlie	L —Lima	U —Uniform
D —Delta	M—Mike	V —Victor
E —Echo	N —November	W—Whiskey
F —Foxtrot	O —Oscar	X —X-Ray
G —Golf	P —Papa	Y —Yankee
H —Hotel	Q —Quebec	Z —Zulu
I —India	R —Romeo	

Transmission of numbers

0 — Zero	4 — Fower	8 — Ait
1 — Wun	5 — Fife	9 — Niner
2 — Too	6 — Six	Thousand — Tousand
3 — Tree	7 — Seven	

Examples of number transmissions are: 10 — Wun Zero; 583 — Fife Ait Tree; 2,500 — Too Fife Zero Zero; 3,000 — Tree Tousand. Frequences are passed in the form: 118.1 — Wun Wun Ait Day-see-mal Wun; 120.375 — Wun Too Zero Day-see-mal Tree Seven (the final digit being omitted).

Q-Code

A further note concerns the Q-Code, now obsolete in aviation, apart from certain enduring terms like QGH, QNH and QFE. This was an expansion of the Q-Code already in use by the merchant marine and it became possible to exchange information on practically all subjects that might be needed in aviation communications. These three letter groups could be sent by Wireless Telegraphy (W/T) in morse with great speed and overcame any inherent language difficulties. For example, an operator would send the code 'QDM' to a ground station, which meant 'What is my magnetic course to steer with zero wind to reach you?' The ground operator would transmit 'QDM' and the appropriate figure.

Standard words and Phrases used in R/T communications

Word/Phrase	**Meaning**
Acknowledge	Let me know that you have received and understood this message.
Affirm	Yes.
Approved	Permission for proposed action granted.
Break	Indicates the separation between messages.
Cancel	Annul the previously transmitted clearance.
Check	Examine a system or procedure (no answer is normally expected).
Cleared	Authorised to proceed under the conditions specified.
Confirm	Have I correctly received the following ...? *or* Did you correctly receive this message?
Contact	Establish radio contact with ... (The obsolete code 'QSY', which meant the same thing, is often still used by pilots.)
Correct	That is correct.
Correction	An error has been made in this transmission (or message indicated). The correct version is ...
Disregard	Consider that transmission as not sent.
How do you read	What is the readability of my transmission?
I say again	I repeat for clarity or emphasis.
Monitor	Listen out on (frequency).
Negative	No *or* permission not granted *or* that is not correct.
Over	My transmission is ended and I expect a response from you.
Out	My transmisison is ended and no response is expected.
Pass your message	Proceed with your message.
Read back	Repeat all, or the specified part, of this message back to me exactly as received.
Report	Pass required information.
Request	I should like to know ... *or* I wish to obtain ...

Roger	I have received all your last transmission. (Note: under no circumstances to be used in reply to a question requiring a direct answer in the affirmative (*affirm*) or negative (*negative*).)
Say again	Repeat all, or the following part of your last transmission.
Standby	Wait and I will call you. (Note: No onward clearance to be assumed.)
Verify	Check and confirm.
Wilco	I understand your message and will comply with it. (Abbreviation for 'will comply'.)

The words *over* and *out* are now rarely used in practice and the original form of *affirmative*, superseded in 1984 by *affirm*, is still to be heard. (Old habits die hard!) Also note that controllers who are recently ex-military, sometimes use standard RAF phrases such as *wait* (for *standby*) and *wrong* (for *correction*).

The clarity of radio transmissions is expressed by the following scale:

Readability 1 — Unreadable;
Readability 2 — Readable now and then;
Readability 3 — Readable but with difficulty;
Readability 4 — Readable;
Readability 5 — Perfectly readable.

Note that controllers in exasperation sometimes use non-standard phrases like 'Strength a half' for really awful radios! Another phrase in common usage is 'Carrier wave only', indicating that an unmodulated transmission is being received by the ground station, ie, it is just noise without the accompanying speech.

Communications

Aeronautical ground stations are identified by the name of the location, followed by a suffix which indicates the type of service being given.

Suffix	**Service**
Control	Area Control Service
Radar	Radar (in general)
Approach	Approach Control
Tower	Aerodrome Control
Ground	Ground Movement Control
Precision	Precision Approach Radar

Information	Flight Information Service
Radio	Aerodrome Air/Ground Communications Service

When satisfactory two-way communication has been established, and provided that it will not be confusing, the name of the location or the callsign suffix may be omitted. The basic rule is that the full callsigns of both stations must be used on the first transmission. For example:

Aircraft: Southend Tower GABCD.

ATC: GABCD Southend Tower pass your message.

Aircraft callsigns may take various forms but they must remain the same throughout the flight. However, if aircraft on the same frequency have similar callsigns ATC may instruct one of them to alter the format temporarily to avoid confusion. One other point is that aircraft in the heavy wake turbulence category must include the word 'heavy' immediately after the callsign in the initial call. This is to remind the controller that increased separation may be necessary for following aircraft.

The recommended methods of presenting callsign are summarised below.

	Example	
Type of callsign	**Full**	**Abbreviated**
(a) The five-character callsign corresponding to the registration marking of the aircraft, the first one or two letters being the national prefix	G–ABCD	GCD
(b) The five-character callsign referred to in (a) above, preceded by the R/T designator of the aircraft operator	British Midland G–BMAE	British Midland AE
(c) The five-character callsign referred to in (a) above, preceded by the type of aircraft (An American practice which is slowly spreading to Europe)	Cherokee G–AWTM	Cherokee TM
(d) The R/T designator of the aircraft operator, followed by the flight identification	Speedbird 835	No abbreviation permitted
(e) Alpha-numerical callsign corresponding with the aircraft registration marking	N786AQ	86AQ

In practice other variations are to be heard, some pilots using their company two-letter designator and flight number rather than the normal company name and flight number, eg WG748 for Air Ecosse 748. Either is correct and it is quite common for controllers, faced with an unfamiliar company designator on a flight progress strip, or simply forgetting what it stands for, to revert, for example, to KG for Orion or LS for Expressair.

The aim is to prevent incidents and potential accidents caused by callsign ambiguities but these still occur in sufficient numbers to cause concern. Regular bulletins of Mandatory Occurrence Reports (MORs) are circulated amongst pilots and controllers and these often contain reports of aircraft with similar callsigns taking instructions meant for each other by mistake.

Up to the mid-sixties airline operators generally used the aircraft registration letters for flight-planning purposes. As the ATC system became more sophisticated and traffic increased, the flight number became the prime means of identification. (On inter-continental flights this practice came into use much earlier.) There were several reasons for the change, one of the more mundane ones being the amount of extra work involved at the ATC Centres if the company had to change the aircraft on a route becaues of unserviceability or other reasons. In those days computer-printed flight progress strips were far in the future, the strips having to be hand-written by the 'A-Man', who acted as assistant to the Airways Controller, based on advance information from the flight plan.

Perhaps BEA might have decided that Vanguard G-APEP was to be replaced on, say, a London-Belfast trip, by G-APEN. Since each UK internal flight on airways might take up to eight flight strips, one for each en route reporting point, there was an awful lot of writing to be done at peak periods. The Airways Controller or 'D-Man', to use the jargon of the day, was not very happy to be given a collection of altered strips, so they all had to be written out again. Speaking from personal experience, the change to flight numbers saved a lot of writer's cramp. Unfortunately, the spotters under Amber 1 or Red 3 would gnash their teeth because they were no longer able to 'cop' (a spotter's jargon for seeing) the entire Vanguard fleet or whatever, without moving from the back garden!

In 1968 the flight plan system was amended to facilitate the introduction of the repetitive flight plan for scheduled services. The use of flight numbers became even more widespread because they were then the only form of identification known sufficiently far in advance of the departure. In the mid-seventies smaller charter operators in the United Kingdom who had formerly used the registration for their Piper Aztecs, Navajos and the like, began to use flight numbers instead. One of the main reasons for this was that many European controllers treated them as private aircraft and gave them low priority, even though they were *bona fide* commercial flights.

This greater use of flight numbers led to more callsign confusion and in 1972 a BEA pilot suggested that the letters of the phonetic alphabet, being more distinctive sounding than the numerals, could be used as a direct replacement for the flight numbers. Using all 26 letters, a callsign containing the company designator followed by three letters could produce over 17,000 different combinations, far more than the 9,999 attainable by the employment of four digits. The idea was that the flight number system would be retained for commercial purposes and the alphabetical equivalent used for ATC only.

However, on further examination by the British Airline Pilots' Association (BALPA), the idea was found to have two significant defects. First, a two-letter designator followed by three other letters would in many cases be identical to a civil registration marking, for example DA-BEC. The second point was that the letters of a callsign equivalent to a particular flight number for one company would also be used for the same flight number by other airlines, so that the similarity would simply be transferred into the new system and identical numbers would still produce identical callsigns.

The solution was to place an extra character, a numeral, in the callsign so as to give it a distinctive appearance and sound, for example Dan-Air Bravo Six Foxtrot Echo. It was indeed Dan-Air which offered to try out the new alpha-numeric callsign on its scheduled domestic services. When the first flight under the new scheme departed from Leeds for Glasgow in October 1972, it went out as DA-B3TF and returned as DA-B3TG.

The new system seemed to work quite well but there were some administrative problems and it was shelved after four days. British European Airways recognised the problem but still would not accept the alphabetic form, although they attempted to use a hybrid in which the second digit of the flight number was deleted and an equivalent suffix letter added. As a system it was far from adequate and created as many problems as it solved. After a six month trial, it too was dropped.

The flight number method remained in use but evidence of its ambiguities continued to be gathered by various research groups. Finally, from 1978, ICAO was persuaded by some of its member states to set up an official study group which used a simulator to prove that controllers and pilots would have little difficulty in coping with alpha-numerics. Dan-Air commenced a further in-flight trial in February 1982 but suspended it in October 1984.

Unfortunately, the new form was not yet incorporated into International Civil Aviation Organisation (ICAO) procedures and so could not be used on international flights without the consent of the states overflown. Dan-Air obtained this consent from Ireland and the Netherlands but France never did decide. Without French participation, the trial could not be extended to include the busy holiday routes to Spain, Portugal and the Canaries, which would also permit other British operators to take part. Hence Dan-Air continued to use conventional flight numbers on its Inclusive Tour (IT) routes.

Brymon Airways had been ready to join the trial since November 1982 but was hindered by the refusal of the British Airports Authority to accept these callsigns at Heathrow. The BAA is apparently wary that this new form of callsign would give it the same problems experienced with two other non-standard forms used by BA Shuttle and British Airtours. These employ random selections of letters in the callsign which are not predictable by any simple mathematical process and therefore are not compatible with computer systems without very expensive software. However, if the full alpha-numeric were used, it could be handled easily by computers because of its mathematical base. One day the system may be adopted universally but, regrettably, it may take a major accident caused directly by callsign confusion to bring this about.

Moving on from callsign presentation, there are certain other basic R/T rules with which pilots must comply. Aircraft flying in controlled airspace must obtain permission from the controlling authority before changing frequency to another station. This is one of the most common causes of acrimony between controllers and pilots; aircraft disappearing from the approach frequency just as a turn or other important instruction is required to be passed. After a brief delay the aircraft comes up on the tower frequency and has to be told to go back to approach. This sort of thing is irritating and can be dangerous. Of course, pilots sometimes take instructions intended for other aircraft, particularly if the callsigns are similar.

Another important point is that an ATC route clearance is not an instruction to take off or enter an active runway. The words *take-off* are used only when an aircraft is cleared for take-off. At all other times the word *departure* is used—the disaster at Teneriffe in 1977 was caused mainly by a flight crew interpreting a route clearance as also implying a take-off clearance. They must have known better but there were pressing distractions and so the fatal error was made.

There is a stringent requirement to read back route (or airways) clearances because of the possible seriousness of a misunderstanding in the transmission and receipt of these messages. If the controller does not receive a read-back, the pilot will be asked to give one. Similarly, the pilot is expected to request that instructions be repeated or clarified if any are not fully understood. The ATC instructions listed below are to be read back in full by the pilot.

Level instructions, heading instructions, speed instructions, airways or route clearances, clearance to enter, land on, take off on, backtrack or cross an active runway, Secondary Surveillance Radar operating instructions, altimeter settings and frequency changes.

Examples are:

ATC: GBFVM cleared to cross Blue 1 at Ottringham Flight Level 180.

Aircraft: Cleared to cross Blue 1 at Ottringham Flight Level 180, GVM.

ATC: GTE contact Castledon Approach 119.65.

Aircraft: 119.65 GTE.

Levels may be reported as altitude, height or Flight Level, according to the phase of flight and the altimeter setting, but a standard form of reporting is adhered to. An aircraft climbs, descends, maintains, passes, leaves or reaches a level, the following ATC instructions clarifying this:

Aer Lingus 920 climb FL 190.

Speedbird 231 report passing FL 160.

Swissair 842 report reaching FL 190.

British Midland 581 maintain 3,500 ft.

Aircraft: WG748 request descent.

ATC: WG748 descend FL 60.

Aircraft: WG748 leaving FL 90 for FL 60.

Sometimes a changing traffic situation may necessitate an intermediate halt to a descent or climb. 'Aer Lingus 920 stop descent FL 150.' Occasionally, for traffic reasons, a higher than normal rate of climb or descent may be requested to avoid eroding separation. 'Aer Lingus 920 climb to FL 190, expedite passing FL 150.'

Separations

The rules for separation of IFR traffic, particularly when radar is not available, are quite complicated and probably of little interest to the layman. Suffice it to say that the basic radar separations are five miles laterally (ten in certain cases) and/or 1,000 ft vertically up to FL 290. Above this level 2,000 ft vertical separation is applied and above FL 450 for supersonic aircraft 4,000 ft is the norm.

For aircraft departing from an airport the minimum separation is one minute, provided the aircraft fly on tracks diverging by 45° or more immediately after take-off. Where aircraft are going the same way, and provided the first has filed a true airspeed (TAS) 40 kt or more faster than the second, the separation is two minutes. With a TAS of 20 kt or more faster than the second aircraft it becomes five minutes and in all other cases it is ten minutes. Radar may reduce some of these times and they are also affected by the demands of vortex wake separation and local procedures.

Control Tower at Sumburgh, Shetland Isles (CAA).

Chapter 3

Types of airspace

Flight Information Region (FIR)

The United Kingdom is divided into two FIRs, the London and the Scottish, the boundary between them being the 55°N line of latitude. Above 24,500 ft these areas are known as Upper Flight Information Regions, abbreviated to UIR. The London FIR comes under the London Air Traffic Control Centre at West Drayton, close to Heathrow, and the Scottish FIR under Scottish ATCC at Atlantic House near Prestwick. Southern Ireland comes under the jurisdiction of the ATCC at Shannon, the stretches of the Atlantic to north and south being controlled by Reykjavik and Shanwick Oceanic Controls, respectively. At Manchester Airport there is an ATC Sub-Centre which controls traffic below 13,000 ft in most of the area once dealt with by the now-defunct Preston ATCC.

Airways

Airways are normally ten miles wide and generally have a base between 3,000 ft and FL 55. With some exceptions they extend virtually to FL 245, the base of upper airspace in Britain. Aircraft flying in them are required to operate under IFR and are separated positively by ATC, using radar or procedural methods. 'Westbound' flights, which could in practice also be on north-west or south-west headings, fly at even thousands of feet and 'eastbound' flights at odd thousands. Some airways are activated for peak periods only, usually weekends and recognised holidays.

Upper airspace

Upper airspace extends from FL 245 up to FL 660 and is designated a Special Rules Area. The Upper Air Routes lie within it, the majority of them following the line of the normal airways below, hence Blue 1 and Upper Blue 1. However, fuel saving requirements in the last decade or so have led to an increasing tendency for aircraft to fly direct routes between radio beacons sometimes several hundred miles apart. Some of these *ad hoc* routeings have resulted in the establishment of UARs to regulate their use.

The whole of the upper airspace is covered by joint civil and military radar units to co-ordinate the large numbers of flights within it. The standard vertical separation above FL 245 is increased to 2,000 ft so that aircraft flying in opposite directions are 4,000 ft apart. This reduces the problem found in the early days of high-level jet transports, when the lack of visual references in the upper atmosphere led to violent evasive action being taken from traffic which the pilot erroneously believed was at the same level.

Terminal Control Areas

As the name implies, these are established around one or more busy airports to protect aircraft descending from an airway into the appropriate Control Zone or, conversely, climbing out of it. The abbreviation for Terminal Control Area is TMA as they were formerly called Terminal Manoeuvring Areas. Their lower limit is around 2,500 ft, the top as high as FL 245, and they connect with airways serving the complex.

Control Zones

Control Zones are found at busy airports, often but not always within TMAs, and extend from ground level up to the base of the TMA. The dimensions are sufficient to enable aircraft to manoeuvre onto final approach without leaving the confines of controlled airspace.

Special Rules Zones

An airspace within an FIR inside which aircraft are required to comply with the instructions of ATC is known as a Special Rules Zone. These extend upwards from ground level to a specified altitude or Flight Level.

Special Rules Areas

A Special Rules Area is similar to an SRZ but extends upwards from a specified altitude or flight level and has an upper limit. They are usually provided to link an SRZ with adjacent airways, for example at Leeds-Bradford and Stansted.

Upper Heyford Mandatory Radio Area

Replacing the Radar Advisory Service Zone, it was introduced by the USAF in a positive attempt to separate the large numbers of

Overleaf: Left *Plan of Military Aerodrome Traffic Zones* (CAA). **Right** *United Kingdom Flight Information and Altimeter Setting Regions* (CAA).

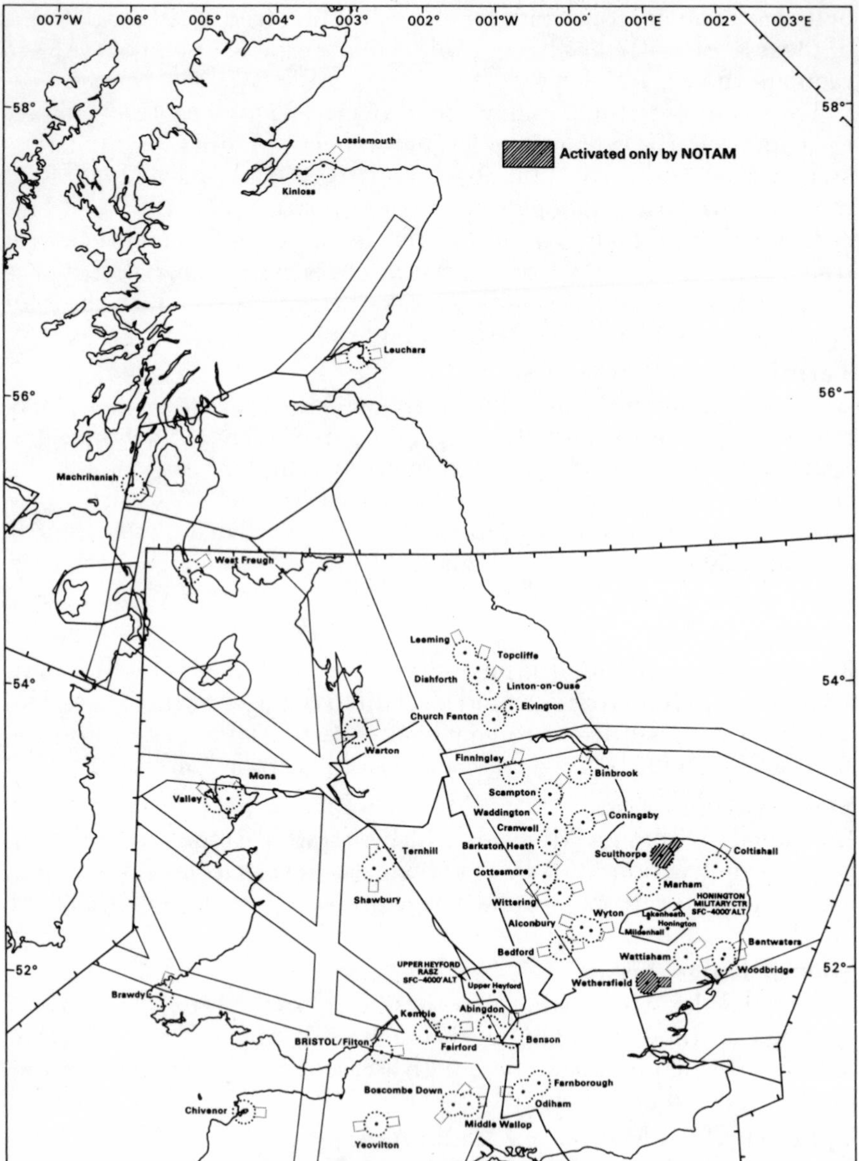

CAA C(G)6 CARTO DO. Drg No.8598 19-4-83 12-5-84

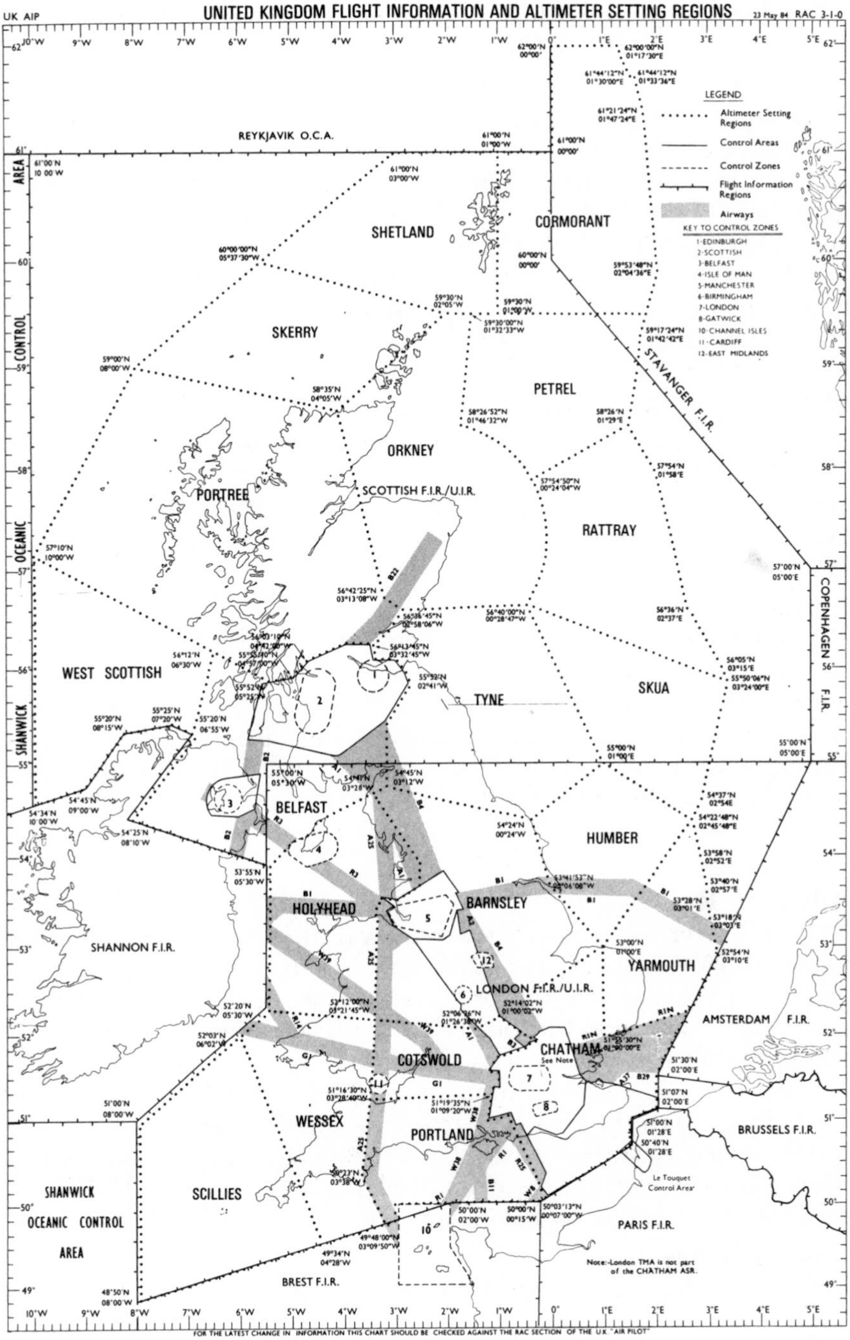
UK AIP
UNITED KINGDOM FLIGHT INFORMATION AND ALTIMETER SETTING REGIONS
23 May 84 RAC 3-1-0
LEGEND
Altimeter Setting Regions
Control Areas
Control Zones
Flight Information Regions
Airways
KEY TO CONTROL ZONES
1-EDINBURGH
2-SCOTTISH
3-BELFAST
4-ISLE OF MAN
5-MANCHESTER
6-BIRMINGHAM
7-LONDON
8-GATWICK
10-CHANNEL ISLES
11-CARDIFF
12-EAST MIDLANDS
REYKJAVIK O.C.A.
SHANWICK OCEANIC CONTROL AREA
SHETLAND
CORMORANT
SKERRY
PETREL
ORKNEY
SCOTTISH F.I.R./U.I.R.
PORTREE
RATTRAY
STAVANGER F.I.R.
COPENHAGEN F.I.R.
WEST SCOTTISH
TYNE
SKUA
BELFAST
HUMBER
HOLYHEAD
BARNSLEY
SHANNON F.I.R.
YARMOUTH
LONDON F.I.R./U.I.R.
AMSTERDAM F.I.R.
CHATHAM
See Note
COTSWOLD
WESSEX
PORTLAND
BRUSSELS F.I.R.
SCILLIES
Le Touquet Control Area
PARIS F.I.R.
BREST F.I.R.
Note:-London TMA is not part of the CHATHAM ASR.
FOR THE LATEST CHANGE IN INFORMATION THIS CHART SHOULD BE CHECKED AGAINST THE RAC SECTION OF THE U.K. "AIR PILOT"

light aircraft operating below 4,000 ft in the South Midlands from high speed jet traffic, mainly F-111s. Radio equipment and compliance with instructions is now compulsory.

Military Aerodrome Traffic Zones

The purpose of a MATZ is to provide a volume of airspace within which increased protection may be given to aircraft in the critical stages of circuit, approach and climb-out. It normally comprises the airspace within five nautical miles radius of the airfield from the surface up to 3,000 ft. In addition, a 'stub' out to five miles protects the final approach path of the most used runway. Although it is not mandatory for civil pilots to request permission to penetrate a MATZ, it is obviously highly desirable for them to do so.

Military Training Areas

Military Training Areas are defined areas of upper airspace, within which intense military flying takes place during weekdays and occasionally, with prior notification, at weekends. Certain airways, including Upper Amber 25 and Upper White 39 are affected when MTAs are active.

Aerodrome Traffic Zones

The dimensions relate to the midpoint of the longest runway and its length. For example, if the longest runway is greater than 1850 metres, the boundary of the ATZ will be a circle of radius 2½ NM from the midpoint of that runway. Aerodromes with shorter runways have smaller ATZs but the vertical limit remains 2,000 feet above aerodrome level. Both within or outside controlled airspace pilots must either avoid the ATZ or obtain permission to fly through it.

Advisory Routes

Normally referred to as ADRs, Advisory Routes have been established where public transport aircraft use certain routes but not in sufficient quantity to justify the full protection of an airway. To distinguish them from airways, the prefix *Delta* for 'discretionary' eg, Delta White 9, Delta Green 22, is used. Most of the ADRs are to be found in Scotland and Northern England with a mere two (Delta Red 8 and Delta Red 37) in the South. A few have achieved sufficient density to reach airway status, one of them being Blue 22, formerly Delta Blue 22, between the Scottish TMA and Aberdeen. Unlike on airways the quadrantal rule is applied for level allocation.

Danger Areas

The most common Danger Areas are weapons ranges but the term

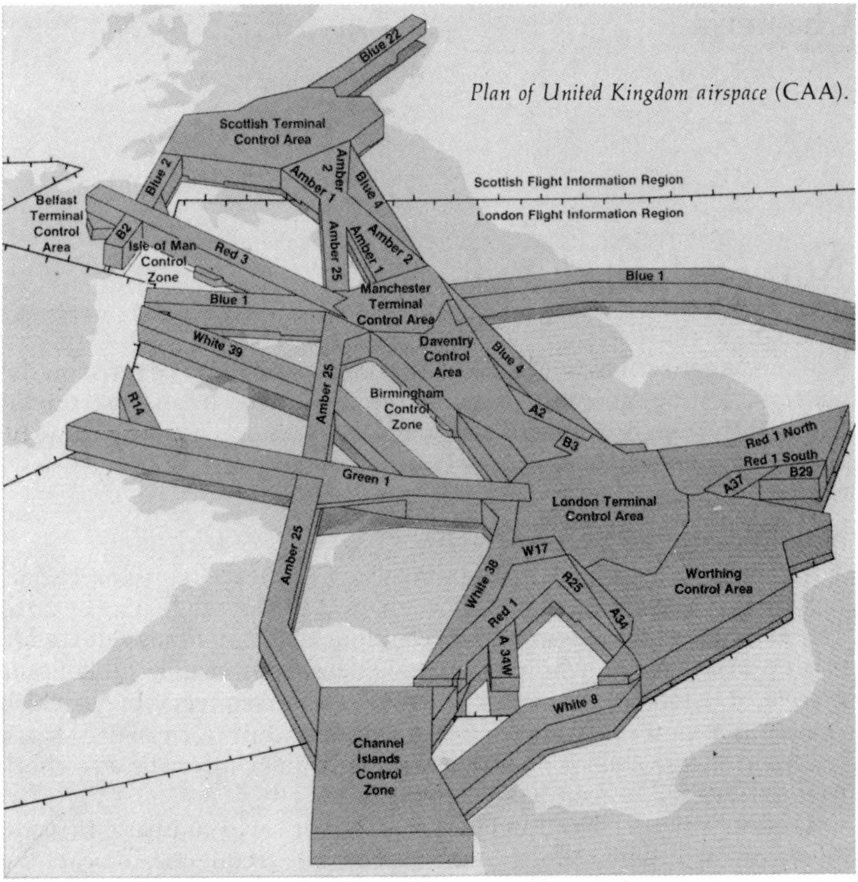

Plan of United Kingdom airspace (CAA).

can also embrace parachuting and other potentially hazardous activities. Radar crossing services are available for some of them.

Prohibited Areas

Most Prohibited Areas are centred on nuclear power stations, over-flight being prohibited below 2,000 ft above ground level within a radius of two miles. Others include the Red Arrows' training area at Scampton in Lincolnshire and a number of sensitive places in Northern Ireland.

Free airspace

Free airspace is the airspace outside the areas listed above, within which aircraft are allowed to fly as they wish without hindrance or radio calls. In instrument conditions pilots are expected to conform to a simple procedure called the quadrantal rule which regulates altitude according to the aircraft's heading.

Chapter 4

Navigational aids

Radio navigational aids assist a pilot in threading his way through the airways, letting down at destination and then, if an Instrument Landing System is installed, following its beam down to the runway. The main types of navaid in the United Kingdom are described briefly below.

Non-Directional Beacon (NDB)

The commonest, and one of the simplest of aids is the Non-Directional Beacon. It is used to mark airways, when its useful range may be up to 100 miles, and as an approach and landing aid, sometimes referred to as a Locator Beacon, when its range will be about 15 miles. It consists merely of a radio transmitter in the medium frequency band which sends out a continuous steady note in all directions. A callsign of three letters in morse code is superimposed at regular intervals as a check that the desired beacon has been tuned in.

The Automatic Direction Finder (ADF), or radio compass, fitted in an aircraft will, when tuned to the appropriate frequency, indicate the relative position of the transmission source by means of a needle on a dial. The great disadvantage of the NDB is that it is very prone to interference. For example a thunderstorm cell in the area will often cause the cockpit needle to point to it in preference to the beacon, not a happy state of affairs!

VHF Omni-Directional Range (VOR)

VORs broadcast their signals in all directions but the signals vary around the compass in such a way that each direction has its own signal which cannot be confused with that of any other direction. If an aircraft receiver can pick-up and decode the signal from a VOR, it can tell the bearing (or radial as it is termed) from the station. As a

Right *ILS Approach Chart for Runway 28 Left at Heathrow* (British Airways Aerad).

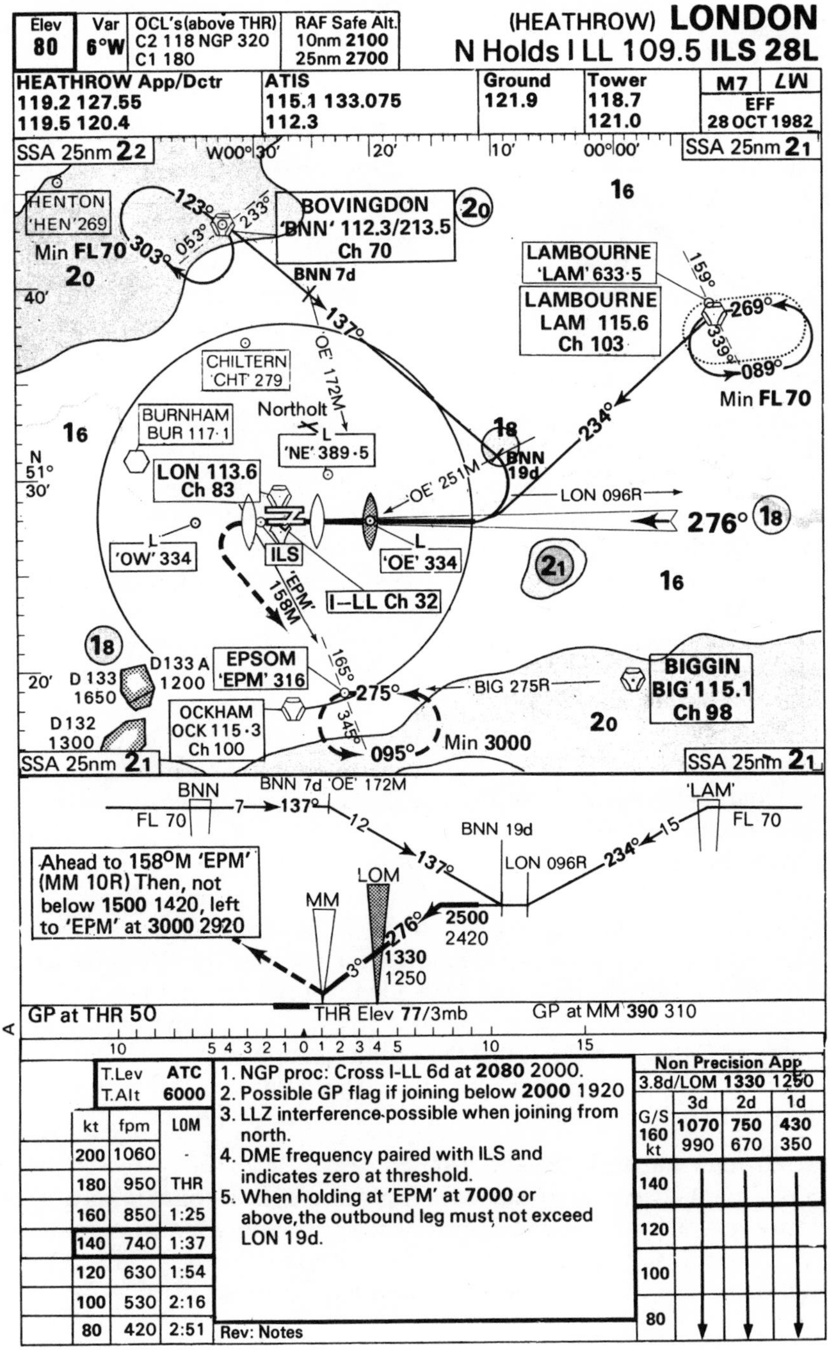
Elev 80
Var 6°W
OCL's(above THR) C2 118 NGP 320 C1 180
RAF Safe Alt. 10nm 2100 25nm 2700
(HEATHROW) LONDON
N Holds I LL 109.5 ILS 28L
HEATHROW App/Dctr 119.2 127.55 119.5 120.4
ATIS 115.1 133.075 112.3
Ground 121.9
Tower 118.7 121.0
M7
EFF 28 OCT 1982
SSA 25nm 22
W00°30′
20′
10′
00°00′
SSA 25nm 21
HENTON 'HEN'269
Min FL70
BOVINGDON 'BNN' 112.3/213.5 Ch 70
BNN 7d
123°
233°
053°
303°
137°
'OE' 172M
LAMBOURNE 'LAM' 633·5
LAMBOURNE LAM 115.6 Ch 103
159°
269°
339°
089°
Min FL70
234°
CHILTERN 'CHT' 279
BURNHAM BUR 117·1
Northolt
'NE' 389·5
LON 113.6 Ch 83
'OE' 251M
BNN 19d
LON 096R
276°
'OW' 334
ILS
'OE' 334
I–LL Ch 32
'EPM' 158M
165°
EPSOM 'EPM' 316
D133 A 1200
D 133 1650
D132 1300
OCKHAM OCK 115·3 Ch 100
275°
345°
095°
BIG 275R
Min 3000
BIGGIN BIG 115.1 Ch 98
SSA 25nm 21
SSA 25nm 21
N 51° 30′
40′
20′
BNN
FL 70
BNN 7d 'OE' 172M
137°
12
BNN 19d
LON 096R
234°
15
'LAM'
FL 70
Ahead to 158°M 'EPM' (MM 10R) Then, not below 1500 1420, left to 'EPM' at 3000 2920
LOM
MM
276°
2500 2420
1330 1250
3°
GP at THR 50
THR Elev 77/3mb
GP at MM 390 310
10
5 4 3 2 1 0 1 2 3 4 5
10
15
T.Lev ATC
T.Alt 6000
1. NGP proc: Cross I-LL 6d at 2080 2000.
2. Possible GP flag if joining below 2000 1920
3. LLZ interference possible when joining from north.
4. DME frequency paired with ILS and indicates zero at threshold.
5. When holding at 'EPM' at 7000 or above, the outbound leg must not exceed LON 19d.
Rev: Notes
Non Precision App
3.8d/LOM 1330 1250
G/S 160 kt
3d 2d 1d
1070 750 430
990 670 350
140
120
100
80

kt	fpm	LOM
		THR
200	1060	-
180	950	THR
160	850	1:25
140	740	1:37
120	630	1:54
100	530	2:16
80	420	2:51

convenience the receiver can add 180° to the 'From' determination and instruct the pilot which way to fly 'To' the station. A 'To/From' flag on the instrument face tells the pilot in which mode it is operating.

Distance Measuring Equipment (DME)

While VOR gives accurate, specific directional information, it cannot make explicit distance measurements. The pilot, however, may find his distance from the station by taking an intersection of radials from two VORs, or by doing a timed radial manoeuvre with a single VOR. A simpler answer is to use DME which is associated closely with VOR, the combination providing an accurate position fix. A special transmitter in the aircraft sends out pulses in all directions and these are received at the DME station on the ground. As each pulse is received an answering pulse is automatically transmitted and this is picked up in the aircraft. It is in fact the reverse of secondary radar (qv).

As the speed of radio waves is constant at 186,000 miles per second, a computer in the aircraft which measures the time interval between the transmission of a pulse and the receipt of the response can convert this time interval into a distance and display it to the pilot in nautical miles. The presentation is either by means of a mechanical meter or increasingly nowadays by LED (Light Emitting Diode) display. In both cases the distance is in miles and tenths. With some equipment, it is also possible for the 'time to go' to the beacon to be displayed.

It should be noted, incidentally, that the height of the aircraft affects the distance measurement; when directly above the station at 36,000 ft the instrument will show the aircraft as still being six miles from it. This is because the DME measures slant range rather than ground distance, but it is of little importance except when very close to the station.

DMEs are normally co-located with VORs and the frequencies of the two installations are 'paired'. For example, the VOR frequency of 112.7 Mhz is always matched by a DME on Channel 74, a VOR on 114-9 by a DME on Channel 96 and so on. This means that aircraft equipment can be arranged so that the selection of a particular VOR frequency automatically means that the related DME channel is selected at the same time.

Instrument Landing System (ILS)

ILS is a pilot-interpreted aid which gives a continuous indication of whether the aircraft is left or right of the final approach track and also its position in relation to an ideal glide path to the runway. The latter is a standard 3°, giving an approximate rate of descent of 300 ft per minute. Certain airfields may have greater angles owing to high ground on the approach or other local considerations.

This information is augmented by marker beacons on the ground showing range; the outer marker at about four miles from touchdown, a middle marker at around 3,500 ft and sometimes an inner marker just short of the runway threshold. As the aircraft passes over them they give an audible signal. The outer marker transmits low-toned dashes, the middle marker alternates dots and dashes on a medium tone and the inner marker transmits dots (six per second) on a high tone. These markers cannot only be heard, they also light up lamps on a marker indicator on the instrument panel. The outer marker lights up a blue lamp, the middle an amber and the inner a clear lamp, each flashing in time with the codes. These signals, transmitted on a standard 75 Mhz, can often be picked up by domestic radios when in the vicinity of an ILS system.

A transmitter with a large aerial array known as the Localiser is sited at the far end of the runway, transmitting its signals on either side of the centreline of the runway and approach. These signals, called blue on the right of the approach path and yellow on the left, overlap in a beam about 5° wide exactly along the approach centreline.

A typical VOR transmitter site (CAA).

A second unit, the glide path transmitter, is sited at the nearer end and slightly to one side of the runway. Aboard the aircraft there is an instrument with two needles, one which pivots from the top of its case, moves like a windscreen wiper and is actuated by the signals from the Localiser and the other which pivots on the left side of the case, moves up and down and is operated by the transmissions from the glidepath aerial. When the two needles are crossed at right angles, the aircraft is lined up perfectly for a landing. Any deviation can rapidly be corrected by an experienced pilot.

Initial approach on to the ILS is normally achieved by Approach Radar, the aim being to place the aircraft on a closing heading of about 30° to the final approach at a range of between seven and nine miles. The aircraft should be at an appropriate altitude so that the glide path can be intercepted from below rather than attempting to 'chase' it from above. The final turn-on can be done by radar direction, but these days it is usually done automatically by coupling the ILS with the autopilot. Where no radar is available a procedural ILS is flown, similar to an NDB approach with the exception that the procedure turn will intercept the ILS and enable the pilot to establish himself on it.

ILSs are divided into three categories as follows:

Cat 1 – Operation down to 60 m decision height with Runway Visual Range in excess of 800 m.

Cat 2 – Operation down to 60 m decision height with RVR in excess of 400 m.

Cat 3 – Operation with no height limitation to and along the surface of the runway with external visual reference during the final phase of landing with RVR of 200 m.

Sub-divisions are Cat 3b with RVR of 45 m and a planned Cat 3c with RVR of zero. They both require guidance along the runway and the latter also to the parking bay. Special lighting is required for Cat 2 and 3 ILSs, together with safeguarded areas around the sensitive aerial systems to avoid fluctuations caused by vehicles or taxying aircraft.

Microwave Landing System (MLS)

The MLS is so-called because it works in the much higher frequency microwave band, as opposed to the VHF band used by ILS. This creates a number of advantages, not the least of which is a high accuracy. This means that all MLS installations will be built to ICAO Cat 3 standards. Instead of the marker beacons associated with ILS, MLS will normally have continuous distance information provided by

Precision DME (P-DME).

In addition, non-standard offset or curving approaches can be made to avoid obstacles or noise-sensitive areas and the glide path is adaptable to high angle approaches by STOL aircraft or helicopters. The CAA Flying Unit is currently evaluating MLS equipment at Stansted and Heathrow (Runway 28R) to gain the technical and operational experience necessary for the approval of future installations in the United Kingdom. A private system has also been installed at Yeovil. Even so, ILS is expected to remain in use until at least 1995.

Decca

The Decca Navigator provides position fixing ability over an area up to about 300 miles around its transmitter by use of a group (or chain) of special long wave transmitters about 70 to 100 miles apart which radiate in unison. The information thus received enables a pen on a moving map display to trace the path of the aircraft over the ground.

Doppler

The Doppler navigation system is self-contained and produces the desired information on position through a measurement of aircraft velocity by means of Doppler radar and measurement of direction by means of a sensor such as a gyro or magnetic compass. The two sets of information are then processed in a computer.

Inertial Navigation System (INS)

This operates independently of ground stations, being based on a computer aboard the aircraft which derives its input from gyroscopic accelerometers. A pre-determined journey can be programmed in, the output of which will direct the autopilot to fly the required tracks. This enables aircraft to fly direct routeings without reference to radio beacons if first requested from, and approved by, ATC.

Transponder

The transponder is not a navigation aid in the true sense, but its use certainly improves the service which ATC is able to give. Like so many other developments, it was born in World War 2 when it became apparent that it would be useful to be able to distinguish between our own aircraft and those of the enemy, as depicted on a radar screen. IFF (Identification Friend or Foe) was invented to meet this need but the basic device, now called a transponder, has become indispensable in civil, as well as military, aviation.

The transponder is a small airborne transmitter which waits until a radar pulse strikes its antenna and then instantly broadcasts, at a different frequency, a radar reply of its own—a strong synthetic echo. Since ordinary 'skin return' (the reflection of the ground radar pulse from the aircraft structure) is sometimes quite weak, especially at great distances or with small aircraft, the transponder helps the radar operator to track targets that might return an echo too weak to display.

The transponder is simple in concept but in practice is a complex, sophisticated device. It is triggered into either of two modes of reply by the nature of the ground radar pulse. Without delving too deeply into the technicalities, Mode A is employed for identification and Mode C for altitude information. (Modes B and D, by the way, are reserved for research and future development.) At the UK Control Centres, radar replies are channelled into a computer which decodes the pulses, converts them into a letter and number display, and places a label alongside the appropriate target on the radar screen. The information includes the callsign and altitude of the aircraft.

This Secondary Surveillance Radar (SSR) has many advantages. One of the most important is that aircraft identification is easy to achieve and eliminates the necessity of requesting a turn of at least 30° from the original heading to confirm which blip is which on the screen. R/T loading is reduced considerably because altitude information is presented continuously to the controller and the pilot no longer needs to make constant checks.

Since the size and attitude of the aircraft in relation to the radar antenna makes no difference to the strength of the radar echo, SSR eliminates one of the short-comings of primary radar, fading and 'blind' areas. For example, many years ago before Manchester Control (or Preston Radar as it was called then) had SSR, Caravelles inbound to Manchester would fade from the radar as they passed a certain level just south of the Congleton beacon and then reappear some miles further on. It was thought the reason was the small frontal area pointing directly at the radar aerial whilst descending, coupled with a phenomenon known as blind velocity fading. It did not seem to happen with other types of aircraft.

To digress, secondary radar differs from primary radar in that the 'echo' returned to the ground station is augmented by an automatic signal triggered from the aircraft's transponder equipment. Interference from weather and other causes is virtually eliminated. This is not the case with primary radar which is not quite the magic eye some of us would believe; it suffers from all sorts of interference.

Depending on the wavelength of a particular radar, weather clutter can swamp the screen with returns from rain or snow. There are ways of removing, or at least reducing, this clutter, but the aircraft echo can be lost too, especially if it is a small one. It is not uncommon therefore to hear a controller say that he is unable to give a radar approach due to rain clutter and offer an alternative, such as an ILS approach.

Ground Proximity Warning System (GPWS)

The Ground Proximity Warning System is not a navigational aid but it provides an audible warning to the pilot if an aircraft experiences any of the following conditions:

(a) An excessive sink rate;
(b) An excessive terrain closure rate;
(c) An altitude loss after take-off or overshoot;
(d) Proximity to terrain when not in the landing configuration;
(e) A deviation below the glide slope.

In the first four conditions, the warning consists of an audible tone and a spoken warning over a cockpit loudspeaker, 'Whoop, whoop. Pull up'. For the last condition the warning 'Glide slope, glide slope' is used. The warning is repeated as long as the conditions exist.

Aircraft Flight Manuals instruct pilots to climb immediately to a level where the warning is no longer being received. If a pilot gets a 'pull up' warning, his recovery action is to establish the power setting and attitude which will produce the maximum climb gradient consistent with the aircraft configuration. If a 'glide slope' warning is received, recovery action is to apply power to regain the ILS glide slope.

Unfortunately, the GPWS is an extremely sensitive piece of equipment and spurious warnings can be caused by several factors. One of these is a sudden variation in terrain, even though it is well below the aircraft. GPWS incidents can occasionally be heard being discussed on air band frequencies.

Flight Checks

Some of the navaids, particularly ILS, require regular check flights to ensure that their performance remains consistent. These checks, normally flown by the CAAFUs HS 748 aircraft, are not as intensive as those made when the equipment was originally brought into service but they are still quite time-consuming.

Chapter 5

Area or Airways Control

Since messages between the Air Traffic Control Centres (ATCCs) and aircraft on the UK airways system are those which are most easily monitored from all parts of the country, this seems a logical point at which to begin. There are two ATCCs, London and Scottish, supported by a Sub-Centre at Manchester. The dividing line between them is latitude 55°N (roughly the Scottish border) and the Sub-Centre handles traffic below FL 130 on the airways around Manchester and over the Irish Sea.

Transmitter/receiver stations are sited at various strategic positions around Britain and linked to the ATCCs by land line. The aim is to achieve a balanced coverage over the whole area with no 'dead' spots. Similarly, the radar stations are 'remoted' on high ground, where possible, to improve range. London ATCC (LATCC) is served by radar heads at Heathrow, Ash near Canterbury, Ventnor on the Isle of Wight, Clee Hill in Shropshire, Burrington, Devon and St Annes near Blackpool. Additional service is provided on a Eurocontrol agency basis from Mount Gabriel in Eire, a station which extends SSR cover out to 15°W in the south-west approaches.

More information on SSR will be found in a separate section of this book but, briefly, the main function of primary radar is to provide aircraft position. Secondary Radar, or SSR, depends for its operation on a transponder carried in the aircraft which, on receipt of pulses from a ground interrogator, will transmit coded reply pulses back to the ground. When these are decoded by the display equipment, they give the Flight Level of the aircraft together with a four-figure identifying number known as a *squawk*. The primary and secondary information received by the radar stations is processed in a common 'plot extractor', converting the basic radar data into digital form and automatically sending the information to the ATCCs over land lines.

At the ATCC display processing equipment employing modern

computer technology is used to decode the combined radar information from several antenna and displays either a manually selected radar station or a composite area mosaic picture. The SSR squawk is paired with the aircraft callsign in the computer and this callsign label is displayed on the screen instead of the code. This enables the controller to match the radar picture with the strips on his flight progress board.

When the mosaic picture is selected at LATCC, the computer divides the London FIR into 16 mile squares, each of which has radar cover from a 'preferred' radar and a 'supplementary' radar. This avoids the blind spots possible if only one radar were in operation. Should the preferred radar fail, the supplementary will take over automatically, information from a third radar head being upgraded in turn to supplement it.

All incoming primary and secondary digital data is continuously recorded and the tapes are kept for 30 days before being erased and reused. The same applies to all ATC radio messages, whether they be Area, Tower or Approach. The purpose of these recordings is to help an investigating authority to build up a picture of the events surrounding an accident or incident.

To facilitate traffic handling, LATCCs airspace is broken up into sectors, each with its own radio frequencies. Aircraft are passed from one sector to the next with co-ordination between the controllers concerned. From mid-evening as traffic decreases, sectors are 'closed down', the frequencies being 'band-boxed', to use the jargon. Hence nothing may be heard on what is in daytime a busy airways frequency. By the early hours the whole FIR may be controlled by only two frequencies. When the morning shift comes on duty the sectors are activated again to meet the new traffic flow.

Before computers came on the scene in British ATC in the 1970s, flight progress strips at the ATCCs were hand-written in vast quantities. Today the system is automated, apart from a shut-off period for computer maintenance in the small hours of the morning, and it would be advantageous to describe briefly what happens when a particular flight leaves, for example, Liverpool for Heathrow.

If the flight is a scheduled one, it will be on a 'stored plan' in the LATCC computer's bulk store file, if not it will be input on a teleprinter at Manchester Sub-Centre. At the appropriate time as programmed into the computer, usually about 40 minutes before Estimated Time of Departure (ETD), warning strips will be printed by flight strip printers at Manchester and at any location at LATCC

Above *Long range airways radar at Heathrow* (CAA).

Left *Plessey AR5 airways radar site at Burrington, Devon* (CAA).

where advance information of the flight is required.

When Manchester receives the actual time of departure from Liverpool, via a direct telephone link, an activation message will be input to the computer via a keyboard. This will generate an update message for the sectors at the Sub-Centre and those sectors at London which have warning strips. Additionally 'live' strips will be printed at any sector or location concerned with the flight that did not have a warning strip. In all cases the computer will have calculated and printed times for en route reporting points based upon the airborne time input at Manchester. The forecast winds at various levels will have been programmed in and thus automatically taken into account.

The flight of an aircraft from Heathrow to Manchester serves as a good example of how traffic is fed through the airways system. When the departing aircraft comes onto the LATCC Departure Radar Controller's frequency and has complied with the minimum noise routeing element of its Standard Instrument Departure, it is started on its climb to cruising level, using radar separation where necessary between it and other arriving, departing or transitting traffic. To ease the task of the Departure Controller in regard to co-ordination with other sectors concerned with the airspace, there is an internal procedure which permits him to climb the aircraft to an arbitrary level of FL 120 without reference to other sectors.

However, before it reaches this Flight Level or, alternatively, when the aircraft is approaching the sector for which the Daventry Sector Controller is responsible, prior co-ordination is carried out. When this has been done, the aircraft is instructed to contact the Daventry Sector (still with the same London Control callsign.)

Daventry Sector continues the aircraft's climb to its cruising level, once again using radar to resolve any conflictions with other traffic. By this time it is also possible to check the computer on the elapsed time between reporting points and, if these deviate by three minutes or more, the estimates for the rest of the flight are revised and a new ETA is passed to Manchester.

As the flight nears the Manchester TMA boundary co-ordination takes place by direct telephone line between Daventry Sector and the TMA Controller. Descent instructions dependent upon the Manchester traffic situation are then issued and the aircraft transferred to the Manchester Control frequency. The Manchester TMA Controller has a radar display similar to that used by the Daventry Sector and, as the aircraft descends into his airspace, its callsign and level will be visible on his screen. He will also have displayed in front of him the flight progress strips generated by the computer which have been updated by any revised estimates. The descent will be continued until the aircraft comes under the jurisdiction of the Manchester Approach Controller and positioned on the ILS as described in the next chapter.

Ideally, traffic is given an uninterrupted climb to cruising level and, from a convenient point, a continuous descent to final approach. In practice, however, the presence of other traffic rarely makes this possible. Traffic climbing to, say, FL 180 may be given an initial limit of FL 120 against conflicting traffic at Fl 130. By the time it is approaching Fl 120, the other aircraft may be well out of the way and the controller will be able to instruct the pilot to continue his climb to the required level. Before the days of SSR height read-outs, the Area Controller in this example would ask the pilot to report passing FL 110 and then would assess the situation with regard to further climb.

Part of the London Air Traffic Control Centre at West Drayton, Middlesex (CAA).

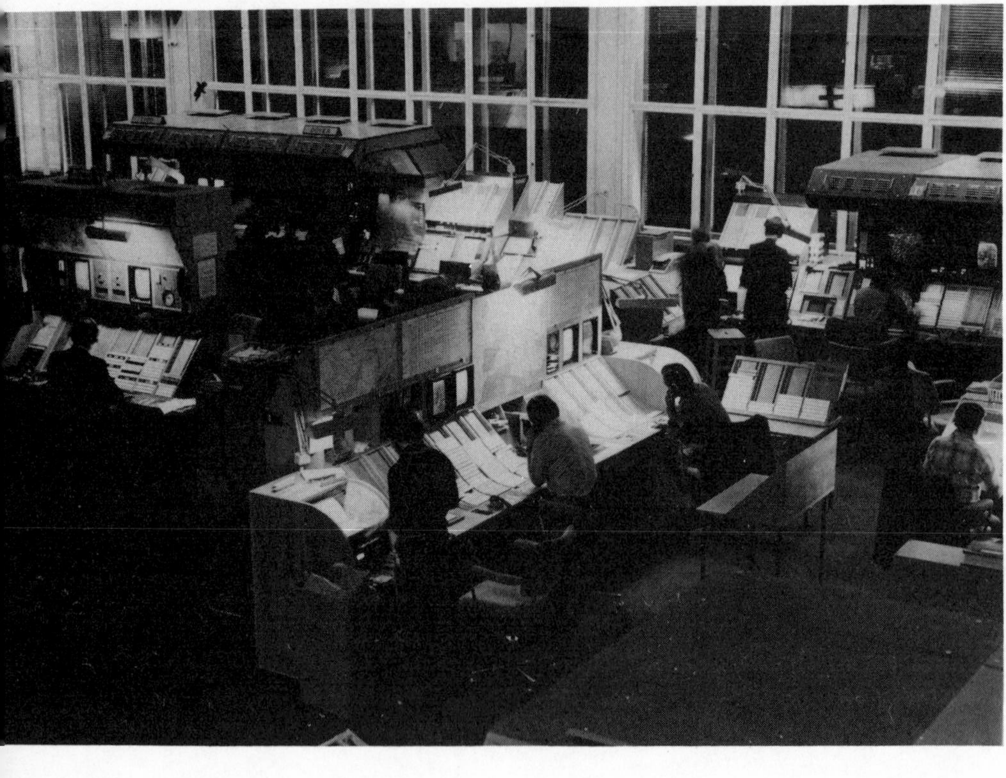

The phraseology used in Area Control is mainly self-evident and some, concerning level changes has already been covered in an earlier chapter. Common phrases to be heard are as follows:

Aircraft: Speedbird 345 request descent.

ATC: Speedbird 345 maintain FL 110 expect descent after Lichfield.

ATC: Air France 045 descend to cross Honiley FL 170 or above. After Honiley descend to FL 130.

The standard airways position report is a little gem of brevity dating back decades to when procedural airways control was first developed. A typical one goes like this:

Aircraft: LC231 Dean Cross 45 FL 90 Pole Hill 10.

This means that the aircraft was over the Dean Cross VOR at time 45, maintaining FL 90 and estimating over the Pole Hill VOR at ten minutes past the next hour.

Nowadays, with comprehensive radar coverage of the airways system, a pilot may be instructed to omit position reports when flying in certain areas, his progress being monitored by the SSR read-out. This reduces the need for R/T considerably.

Certain phrases concerning the operation of transponders are listed below. Since SSR in the United Kingdom is confined mainly to the ATCCs, they will most commonly be heard on airways frequencies. Few Approach Control units have SSR capability as yet, but the number is slowly increasing. The use of the word *squawk*, by the way, seems to have been inspired by the wartime instruction to operate the IFF, (Identification, Friend or Foe), 'Make your cockerel crow' and the pilot's confirmation that the IFF was switched off after landing 'Cockerel strangled.'

Phrase	**Meaning**
Squawk (code)	Set the code as instructed.
Confirm squawk	Confirm the code set on the transponder.
Recycle	Reselect assigned code.
Squawk ident	Operate the special position identification feature.
Squawk low	Select 'low sensitivity' feature.
Squawk normal	Select normal feature.
Squawk standby	Select the standby feature.
Squawk Charlie	Select altitude reporting feature.
Stop Squawk Charlie	Deselect altitude feature.
Verify level	Check and confirm your level. (Used to verify the accuracy of the Mode C derived level information displayed to the controller.)

Chapter 6

Approach Control

An arriving aircraft is transferred from Area to Approach Control at a specified release point. This is not obvious from R/T transmissions because it is passed by land line between controllers shortly before the aircraft comes on to the approach frequency. It may be a position, time or level. The transfer of control is made deliberately flexible to react to differences in the flow of traffic. For example, if the release is 'out of FL 50' the Approach Controller may not alter the heading of the aircraft until he has received a 'passing FL 50' report. The reason for this is that Area Control may have been separating the inbound aircraft from other traffic above FL 50.

Ideally, the arriving aircraft should be released in plenty of time to enable it to carry out a straight-in approach and at the same time to lose height. However, should a busy traffic situation exist, it might be necessary to put it into a holding pattern based upon a radio beacon. The release would then be at a specified level in the holding stack. The holding patterns are a standard oval 'racetrack', the direction of turn and headings being published in navigational charts or approach plates.

At airfields without radar, traffic is separated by procedural methods, the first aircraft making an instrument approach from, say, 3,000 ft, aircraft continuing to hold above at 1,000 ft vertical intervals. As soon as the first aircraft reports visual with the ground or approach lights, and there is a reasonable likelihood of a successful landing, the second aircraft is cleared for the approach and so on. If the aircraft carries out a missed approach prior to becoming visual, it must climb to the safe terrain clearance altitude, in this instance 3,000 ft. Hence it is not hard to see why this altitude is left vacant at the beacon until the first aircraft breaks cloud.

The decision height is the level at which the pilot on an instrument approach must carry out a missed approach if he fails to achieve the required visual reference to continue the approach to a landing. In accordance with ICAO procedures, a major revision of obstacle clearance criteria is being undertaken by the CAA. The revision involves re-calculation of the obstacle clearance heights for all existing approach aids and will be implemented on an aerodrome by aerodrome basis. Therefore it will be several years before all UK aerodromes have the new criteria. The main changes involved are the introduction of an obstacle clearance height and aircraft categories related to speed.

The present obstacle clearance limit—the minimum safe height to which an aircraft may descend either on an instrument approach or in the event of a missed approach—will be replaced by an obstacle clearance height. This will be published on the approach charts for each airfield, aircraft being divided into five speed-related categories, resulting in a reduction of the obstacle clearance heights for the more manoeuvrable types.

Without boring the reader too much with the technicalities, the current term decision height will in future only relate to ILS or MLS approaches. A new phrase, minimum descent height, will be introduced, associated only with what are defined as non-precision approaches like VOR, NDB and radar.

The obstacle clearance criteria are, of course, tied in with company minima for visibility and cloud base, below which a public transport flight is not allowed even to attempt an approach. So far, there are no such statutory provisions for non-public transport flights. However, recommended minima are published for the approach aids at each airfield for the guidance of pilots and these will be passed on R/T when conditions demand.

The term Expected Approach Time is often heard at non-radar equipped airports. This indicates to a pilot that if he has a radio failure he must not commence an instrument approach until this specific time to allow preceding aircraft to descend and land. 'No delay expected' means that a pilot can begin his approach as soon as he reaches the beacon. If his estimate for the beacon is 12, the next aircraft's EAT will be 19, the third's 26 and so on.

A standard seven minutes is assumed to complete the let-down procedure and three minutes will be added to this if an aircraft arrives from certain points of the compass and has to realign itself in the correct direction for the descent. The controller will calculate the figures and update them as necessary. They are often somewhat arbitrary, it being better to over-estimate the EAT and then subsequently make it earlier, a good psychological move!

Pilots' interpretations of instrument let-downs vary enormously, the seven minute standard ranging from five to ten or more, depending upon wind strength, aircraft performance and other factors. One other phrase used in connection with EATs is the rarely heard 'delay not determined.' This is used to meet certain eventualities, such as a blocked runway, when it is not known how long an aircraft may have to hold.

Where Approach Radar is in use, as well as giving a release, the ATCC also transfers radar identity in what is called a handover (a 'handoff' to the Americans). The Approach Controller is thus certain that the aircraft he is directing is the correct blip. The object is to pass headings (vectors) to the pilot to enable him to lock onto the ILS beam by the shortest practicable route commensurate with losing height. If there is no ILS, a Surveillance Radar Approach (SRA) will be given or, when the weather is suitable, radar positioning to a visual final.

In effect a radar directed circuit is flown, the terms downwind, base leg and final (see page 82) all being used where necessary, although the area of sky covered is far bigger than in the normal visual traffic pattern. A closing heading of about 30° is recommended so that when the aircraft intercepts the ILS only a gentle turn is necessary to lock on. The aim is to intercept the standard 3° glide path at approximately 7 to 8 miles out on the extended centreline of the runway. As a 3° glide path is roughly equal to 300 ft of descent per mile, the aircraft should be between 2,000 ft and 2,500 ft at this point.

Subsequent landing aircraft are vectored not less than five miles behind, or further depending upon the vortex wake category of the preceding traffic (See Chapter 13). Bigger gaps may also be built in to give space for departing aircraft at single-runway airports. At certain locations, Heathrow for example, reduction of the separation to 3 miles is authorised to ensure maximum utilisation of the arrival runway. The vortex rules still apply of course. It is quite an art to arrange traffic in line astern with the correct spacing, particularly at Heathrow where four holding stacks serve the airport. Speed control is also used extensively to even out the flow, a minimum of 170 kt being permissible for jets and 160 kt for large propellor-driven aircraft. It is not uncommon to see a slow turbo-prop aircraft only lowering its wheels on short final at Heathrow so as to keep the speed up as long as possible. (According to the book, any speed restriction must be lifted at 4 miles on final approach, but pilots often press on to help the traffic flow.) Within the TMAs during the intermediate stages of the approach, a speed limit of 250 kt is imposed on all traffic to make the

Radar Controller's task a little easier.

The Approach Controller passes an 8 mile check on intercom to his colleague in the Tower who will already have details of the arriving aircraft. If there are no pending departures at the runway holding point, a landing clearance may be given at this point but it is more usual to give this at the 4 mile range, approximately equal to the outer marker on the ILS. Alternatively, once the pilot reports established on the ILS, Approach may tell him to 'Contact the Tower and report passing the outer marker.'

Pilots expect to receive a landing clearance at around 4 miles on final approach, but this is not always possible owing to departing traffic or a previous landing aircraft being slow to clear the runway. Two miles is the absolute minimum for large transport aircraft because an

Standard Terminal Arrival Chart for Manchester (CAA).

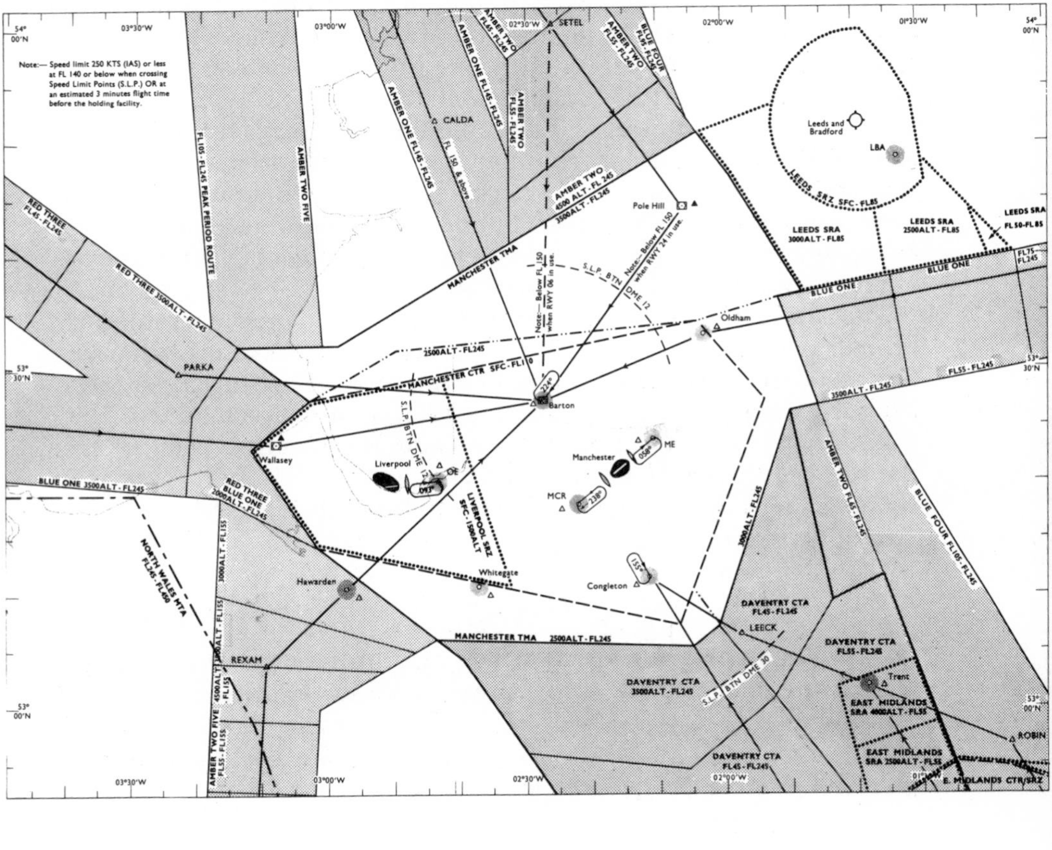

overshoot is a fairly major operation. The phrase 'expect late landing clearance' is sometimes heard because light aircraft in a busy circuit may, of necessity, receive a very late landing clearance. They may even be told to go around if they get too close to the one in front.

For a runway not equipped with ILS the Radar Controller is normally able to offer a Surveillance Radar Approach. If the weather is poor this can be down to ½ mile from touchdown, assuming that the radar is approved for this purpose. With certain types of radar, approaches to 2 miles only may be allowed. This ensures a reasonable chance of seeing the approach lights and making a successful landing in all but the worst weather.

Where only one Approach Controller is on duty and the ILS fails, he may be unable to offer a ½ mile SRA because of the necessity for continuous transmissions during the last 4 miles of the approach. This of course means that any other traffic cannot communicate with him until the talk-down is complete. If a second controller is available, the first can do a ½ mile SRA on a discrete frequency while his colleague continues to sequence traffic onto long final for handover as soon as the preceding aircraft has completed its approach.

SRAs to 2 miles, however, do not require continuous transmissions and the controller can talk to other traffic as necessary, although he must time his calls so that range checks and the associated advisory heights are passed at the correct intervals. The differences between ½ mile and 2 mile SRAs are apparent when one compares the respective phraseology.

The advisory heights are based upon a glide path of 3°, therefore, at 6½ miles the aircraft should be a height of 2,000 ft. Some airfields have non-standard glide path angles because of local obstructions, the advisory heights being adjusted accordingly. It is assumed that the aircraft is flying on QFE, but if the pilot advises that he is using QNH the runway threshold elevation is added to the advisory heights and rounded up to the next 25 ft, the term 'altitude' being used in place of 'height' where necessary.

Phraseology for SRA terminating at ½ mile from touchdown

During the Intermediate Procedure	*This will be a Surveillance Radar Approach, terminated at ½ mile from touchdown. Check your minima, and missed approach point.*

If a change of frequency is required for final approach	*Contact ... on* (frequency) *for final approach. After landing contact Tower on ...* (frequency.)
Before commencing final descent	*Check your wheels down and locked.*
To alter course of aircraft	*Turn left/right* (... degrees) *heading ...*
Azimuth information	*Closing* (final approach) *track from the left/right. Your heading* (of ...) *is good. Slightly left/right of track.*
Approaching $6\frac{1}{2}$ miles from touchdown	*Approaching $6\frac{1}{2}$ miles from touchdown—begin your descent to maintain a 3° glide path.*
At 6 miles from touchdown	*Range 6 miles—height should be 1,850 ft.*
At $5\frac{1}{2}$ miles from touchdown	*Range $5\frac{1}{2}$ miles—height should be 1,700 ft.*
No landing clearance received by 2 miles from touchdown	*Go around—I say again, go around—climb on heading ... to ... ft.* (Further instructions.) *Acknowledge.* (The reason for overshooting is to be given as soon as convenient.)
If during the latter stages of the approach, an aircraft reaches a position from which it appears to the controller that a successful instrument approach cannot be completed	According to circumstances, EITHER: *If unable to proceed visually, go around—climb on heading ... to ... ft.* (Further instructions.) *Over.* OR: *Go around—I say again, go around—climb on heading ... to ... ft.* (Further instructions.) *Acknowledge.* OR: *Climb immediately, I say again, climb immediately on heading ... to ... ft.* (Further instructions.) *Acknowledge.*
At 5 miles from touchdown	*Range 5 miles—height should be 1,550 ft.*
At $4\frac{1}{2}$ miles from touchdown	*Range $4\frac{1}{2}$* miles*—height should be 1,400 ft.*
At 4 miles from touchdown	*Range 4 miles—height should be 1,250 ft. —do not reply to further instructions.*
Landing Clearance (Normally passed between 4 and 2 miles from touchdown)	*Cleared to land runway ...* (Surface wind also given if necessary.)
At $3\frac{1}{2}$ miles from touchdown	*Range $3\frac{1}{2}$ miles—height should be 1,100 ft.*
At 3 miles from touchdown	*Range 3 miles—height should be 950 ft.*
At $2\frac{1}{2}$ miles from touchdown	*Range $2\frac{1}{2}$ miles—height should be 800 ft.*

At 2 miles from touchdown	*Range 2 miles—height should be 650 ft. Check minimum descent height.*
At 1½ miles from touchdown	*Range 1½ miles—height should be 500 ft.*
At 1 mile from touchdown	*Range 1 mile—height should be 350 ft.*
At ½ mile from touchdown	*Range ½ mile from touchdown—approach completed. Out.*
Avoiding action or breaking off approach on instructions from Approach/Aerodrome Control	*Turn left/right ... degrees heading ... climb to ... ft—acknowledge.*

Phraseology for SRA Terminating at 2 miles from touchdown

During the Intermediate Approach	*This will be a Surveillance Radar Approach, terminated at 2 miles from touchdown. Obstacle Clearance Limit ... ft* (above aerodrome/threshold elevation). *Check your minima and missed approach point.*
If a change of frequency is required for final approach	*Contact ... on* (frequency) *for final approach.*
Before commencing final descent	*Check your wheels down and locked.*
To alter course of aircraft	*Turn left/right* (... degrees) *heading ...*
Azimuth information	*Closing* (final approach) *track from the left/right. Your heading* (of ...) *is good. On track. Slightly left/right of track.*
Approaching 6½ miles from touchdown	*Approaching 6½ miles from touchdown—begin your descent to maintain a 3° glide path.*
At 6 miles from touchdown	*Range 6 miles—height should be 1,850 ft.*
At 5 miles from touchdown	*Range 5 miles—height should be 1,550 ft.*
At 4 miles from touchdown	*Range 4 miles—height should be 1,250 ft.*
Landing Clearance (Normally passed between 4 and 2 miles from touchdown)	*Cleared to land Runway ...* (Surface wind also given if necessary.)
At 3 miles from touchdown	*Range 3 miles—height should be 950 ft.*
At 3 miles, or any convenient point during the approach	*Advise when runway/approach lights in sight. Check minimum descent height. After landing contact ... on ...* (frequency).
At 2 miles from touchdown	*Range 2 miles—height should be 650 ft. I cannot assist you further.*
If the pilot has not reported lights in sight	*Continue the approach, or go around at your discretion.*

Avoiding action or breaking off approach on instructions from Approach/Aerodrome Control	*Turn left/right . . . degrees, heading . . . climb to . . . ft.* (Further instructions.)
No landing clearance received by 2 miles from touchdown	*Go around—I say again, go around—climb on heading . . . to . . . ft.* (Further instructions.) *Acknowledge.*

Approach Control Phraseology

Since all major airports now use radar to direct their traffic, I shall deal with this aspect first. An aircraft must be identified before it can receive a radar control or advisory service, in other words, the controller must be sure that one particular blip on his screen is the aircraft that he is directing. This is simple with a radar handover from another ATC unit or by means of SSR, but at airfields outside controlled airspace, where aircraft may approach from random directions with no prior notification, a standard procedure is observed.

ATC: GVM report heading and level.

Aircraft: GVM heading 140 at 2,500 ft.

ATC: GVM for identification turn left heading 110.

The identification turn must be at least 30° different from the original heading. When the pilot reports steady on the new heading, and the controller is sure that he has related the correct blip on his screen with the aircraft, he transmits: 'GVM identified 12 miles south of (airfield)'.

The service to be given is then added.

ATC: This will be radar vectoring to a visual approach runway 23, nominal glide path angle 3°, obstacle clearance limit 320 ft. Check your minima.

(The weather and pressure settings are then passed as a separate transmission.)

If in the initial call the aircraft makes the turn requested and is still not observed on the radar, perhaps because it is out of range, in weather clutter, or below cover, the controller will say 'GVM not identified. Resume own navigation.' D/F will then be used to home the aircraft towards the airfield for eventual radar pick-up.

When identified, the aircraft will be vectored, that is given headings to steer to fit it into the approach sequence or, if traffic is light, direct to final approach. Outside controlled airspace the aircraft may be vectored around unidentified traffic. Information will be given by use of the twelve hour clock, twelve o'clock being straight ahead, three o'clock over the pilot's right shoulder and so on. The distance and relative direction of movement is also given, together with any information on speed, type of aircraft if known, etc. Typical traffic information is passed in this form, 'VF8044 unknown traffic ten o'clock, five miles crossing left to right, fast moving.'

If the pilot does not have the traffic in sight he may request avoiding action. This may, in any case, be initiated by the controller if he considers it necessary. Sometimes rapid action is required to avert the risk of collision: 'VF8044 avoiding action turn left immediately heading 110'. A few incidents have occurred where, by using a too relaxed tone of voice, the controller failed to convey to the pilot the urgency of the required action and the pilot's more leisurely response led to an awkward situation which might have been averted. The CAA eventually instructed all controllers to ensure that their tone of voice does not lull a pilot into a false sense of security.

At locations with no radar, procedural methods are used. The same applies when radar is normally available but unserviceable or seriously affected by weather clutter, or if the pilot wishes to carry out a procedural approach for training purposes. On transfer from the ATCC, the first call will go something like this:

Aircraft: Inverness Approach Loganair 916 descending to FL 60, estimating INS at 42.

ATC: Loganair 916 cleared for beacon approach descend 4,500 ft. Report beacon outbound.

Subsequent reports will be made when 'base turn complete' and, if the beacon is several miles out on final approach, rather than on the airfield, a 'beacon inbound' call will be made as well. These standard calls help the Tower Controller to plan his traffic, bearing in mind that there may be no radar to give him ranges from touchdown.

Where the airport is equipped with ILS, permission to make a procedural approach is given thus: 'GMB cleared ILS approach runway 27, report outer marker outbound QFE 1008'. Subsequent exchanges would be:

Aircraft: GMB outer marker outbound.

ATC: GMB report established ILS inbound. (The phrase 'report procedure turn complete' may be substituted.)

Aircraft: GMB established ILS inbound.

ATC: GMB report outer marker.

Aircraft: GMB outer marker.

ATC: GMB contact Tower 118.1

In good weather, by day or night, even though nominally flying IFR, a pilot may request permission to make a visual approach. This may be granted subject to certain provisos, the most important of which is that the pilot must have the airfield in sight and a reasonable assurance exists that he will be able to complete the landing visually. Standard separation continues to be applied between this aircraft and other arriving and departing traffic. During daylight hours only, IFR flights may be cleared to approach maintaining VMC and their own separation, if reports indicate that this is possible.

It remains for me to mention the QGH, a military procedure which is only available at a handful of civil airfields, usually where a University Air Squadron is based. The QGH dates back to World War 2 but is, nevertheless, highly effective in bringing aircraft safely down to a position from which an approach can be continued visually. This particular Q-Code meant 'Controlled descent through cloud' and uses a cathode ray tube VDF to home the aircraft to the overhead at a safe altitude. Subsequent bearings bring it down a safety lane onto final approach. During the procedure, the pilot's replies are used to obtain D/F bearings and additional transmission may be requested using the words 'Transmit for D/F.' Immediately the aircraft has passed overhead the VDF aerial, turn instructions are given to get it onto the outbound track:

ATC: V91 D/F indicates that you have passed overhead. Turn left heading 120. Report steady.

On completion of the overhead turn and when bearings indicate that the aircraft is outbound, heading corrections derived from a series of bearings are given by the controller as required to make good the outbound track. Descent instructions and the appropriate pressure settings are also given at this point. 'V91 descend to 1,000 ft QFE 1006, report level'. The controller times the outbound leg with a stop watch (usually three minutes) and then gives the aircraft a turn onto a heading to intercept the final approach track. Further D/F checks ensure that it remains within the safety lane and the pilot is told to descend to decision height and report airfield in sight.

The civilian counterpart of the QGH is the VDF Approach which is virtually the direct opposite, in that the pilot interprets the QDM information, rather than the controller. VDF approaches are uncommon these days, reflecting the greater availability of radar and ILS. Apart from this they require a lot of practice by the pilot to perfect them and were never very popular!

Chapter 7

Aerodrome Control

The Aerodrome Controller's function is defined as the issuing of information and instructions to aircraft to achieve a safe, orderly and expeditious flow of traffic and to assist pilots in preventing collisions between:

(a) Aircraft in flight in the vicinity of the aerodrome traffic zone
(b) Aircraft taking off or landing
(c) Aircraft moving on the apron
(d) Aircraft and vehicles, obstructions and other aircraft on the manoeuvring area (ie, the runways and taxyways)

The apron may also come under the jurisdiction of the marshaller, who makes sure that aircraft are parked in the required places. This is particularly important at airports where all or part of the apron is out of sight of the tower. At larger airports, self-manoeuvring markings are painted on the concrete to guide pilots to the stand which he has been allocated on R/T, thus obviating the need for 'the man with the bats'. It would be impossible to control all the service vehicles moving about the apron so these are confined, as far as possible, to lanes outlined in white paint. Airfield fire and maintenance vehicles which need to go on runways and taxyways are controlled on a UHF domestic frequency. At some airfields the Tower frequency may be used for this.

To smooth the running of the larger airports, it may be necessary to split the duties of Aerodrome Control into Air Control and Ground Movement Control (referred to as GMC). The latter's responsibility covers aircraft moving on the apron and aircraft and vehicles on the manoeuvring area, except on runways and their access points. R/T loading at Heathrow necessitates a further sub-division of GMC named Delivery, on which clearances and other information is passed.

Apart from the 'Mark 1 eyeball' and a pair of binoculars, the Tower Controller has few aids. The most useful, but installed at very few places, is the Distance From Touchdown Indicator, colloquially known from its initials as a 'Dufftyscope'. It is a small daylight-viewing cathode ray tube, its picture being derived from the main approach radar, showing the final approach line out to about ten miles.

At airports with only one runway and a high movement rate, Manchester and Gatwick for example, it is invaluable in judging whether or not there is sufficient room to clear a departing aircraft to take off or to allow an aircraft in the circuit to turn in ahead. The Radar Controller is required to give 8 mile and 4 mile checks for traffic on final approach to his colleague in the Tower. The aim is to confirm landing clearance at about 4 miles but certainly at not less than 2 miles.

Runway occupancy is governed by the following rules:

(a) An aircraft shall not be permitted to begin take-off until the preceding departing aircraft is seen to be airborne or has reported 'airborne' by R/T and all preceding landing aircraft are clear of the runway in use.

(b) A landing aircraft will not be permitted to cross the beginning of the runway on its final approach until a preceding departing aircraft is airborne.

There is, however, a phrase 'land after' which seems to puzzle some pilots who probably think it is a place in Wales! Its purpose is to increase runway utilisation by permitting a landing aircraft to touch down before a preceding aircraft which has landed is clear of the runway. The onus for ensuring adequate separation is transferred from controller to pilot. The provisos for this are:

(a) The runway is long enough to allow safe separation between the two aircraft and there is no evidence to indicate that braking may be adversely affected.

(b) It is during daylight hours.

(c) The controller is satisfied that the landing aircraft will be able to see the preceding aircraft which has landed, clearly and continuously until it is clear of the runway.

(d) The pilot of the following aircraft is warned.

There is one other runway procedure which is authorized only at Heathrow and Gatwick where arriving aircraft are 'cleared to land after' (the phrase also being unique). Certain conditions must be met and the procedure is also allowed behind departing traffic.

At some airfields the Tower and Approach function may be combined on one frequency. This is perfectly satisfactory with light to medium traffic flows, but on busy weekends the R/T congestion can be serious, pilots having difficulty in getting a word in edgeways.

Airfields outside controlled airspace possess an Aerodrome Traffic Zone, through which flight is prohibited without a clearance. The circuit direction is a standard left hand, although this may vary for different runways to avoid overflying built-up areas, hospitals and the like. The reason for the left hand pattern is said to date back to the First World War when aircraft like the Sopwith Camel turned much more easily to the left than the right, owing to the torque effect of the rotary engine. When larger aircraft with side-by-side seating were introduced, the pilot sat on the left and this has become traditional. In helicopters, however, this is reversed!

Circuit height is normally 1,000 ft, but at airfields such as Manchester-Barton it is 800 ft, which sometimes leads to confusion when trainee pilots land elsewhere. These days, some pilots tend to fly enormous 'bomber circuits', much to the annoyance of ATC and other aircraft in the circuit.

The circuit is divided into four legs; crosswind, downwind, base, and final approach. The first aircraft to report downwind will be told to 'report final'. ('Number one' may be added to this.) The second will be told 'Number two, follow the Cherokee on base', and so on. If the circuit is very busy the Tower may instruct a pilot to 'report before turning base, four aircraft ahead.' When he does this he will be given an update on his position in traffic, there perhaps being only two ahead by this time.

The standard circuit-joining procedure is to arrive overhead the field at 2,000 ft, descend on the dead side, ie the one opposite the live downwind leg and let down to 1,000 ft. Whilst watching for departing traffic, the pilot then joins the crosswind leg over the upwind end of the active runway. (Wags should note that there is a cemetery under the dead side at Cambridge Airport.)

This should ensure that a joining aircraft does not conflict with one just airborne, as there have been numerous cases in the past of collisions because of careless rejoins a mile or so off the end of the runway. Of course a fast climber like a Rockwell 680 can easily be at 1,000 ft by the time it reaches the end of a longish runway, so it is up to the Tower to make sure that a joining aircraft does not cross its path.

Scheduled and other large aircraft are usually fed straight into the final approach, which can sometimes be tricky. One way to achieve this safely if there is circuit traffic, is to instruct the trainer to continue downwind until he has the arriving aircraft in sight and then follow it. The other solution is an orbit—a 360° turn—always away from the final approach, to be continued until the traffic is sighted. The first method has the disadvantage that a strong tailwind may carry the aircraft into the next county, with perhaps an inexperienced pilot losing sight of the aerodrome. An orbit may be impracticable because of following traffic in the circuit. There is a limit to the number of aeroplanes you can orbit safely in a circuit!

If things are particularly congested and large aircraft are expected, trainers can always be told to land and taxi back to the holding point to await further take-off clearance. Another complication is vortex wake, a phenomenon once referred to as slipstream or propwash, but now known to be a rapidly revolving cylinder of air from each wingtip. This can be so violent that it can overcome the control forces of a following aircraft and invert it. Aircraft in the United Kingdom are placed in four categories depending upon maximum total weight at take-off. These are heavy, medium, small and light. More details are to be found below.

Helicopter operations are less of a problem than might be imagined; the main one being crossing the active runway. However they can clear it quickly and can thus be slotted between arriving and departing aircraft, remaining below 500 ft until clear of the traffic zone. The same applies to their arrival, although at places like Liverpool with an adjacent wide river, pilots are understandably reluctant to approach or depart at low level. In this case, the normal procedure is to change the direction of the circuit traffic away from the helicopter.

Overflying helicopters are treated like any other crossing traffic, either cleared overhead above 2,000 ft if the circuit is busy, or asked to report a few miles away and given traffic information so that they can fly through the pattern without conflict.

The Aerodrome Controller is, of course, pre-warned of arriving traffic by Approach or at some places he handles both functions on the same frequency. Similarly, for departing IFR aircraft he will have the flight progress strips on his pending board, made up when the flight plan was filed with ATC.

At certain busy airports pilots on VFR flights, local, landing away or circuits, are required to 'book out' over the telephone with ATC, giving brief details. This is particularly important with circuit training as the Tower Controller may refuse to accept more than a certain number, dependent upon weather conditions, scheduled traffic, existing congestion and other factors. At smaller airfields, pilots merely call for taxi clearance from the parking area stating their requirements. Training flights are often referred to by the word 'detail' as in 'Coventry Tower GAXVW request taxy clearance, two on board circuit detail.' This is a throwback to military jargon, as is the term 'fanstop' for a practice engine failure after take-off.

Aircraft on IFR flight plans should first request permission to start engines so that ATC can warn of any likely delays and thus minimise fuel wastage. If there is no delay, 'Start up approved' is passed, together with the outside air temperature in degrees Celsius. The QNH, QFE and runway in use may also be given in the same transmission, although this is optional. The alternative is to pass them when taxy clerance is given. In practice, pilots often call in advance for this 'airfield data', acknowledge it and say 'call you again for start'.

Traffic on the congested holiday routes to the Mediterranean and other parts of Europe is subject to complex rules known as departure flow regulation. They require the aircraft to take off at a specified time, ATC being allowed six minutes over and above this to cover any taxying delays or short waits for landing traffic. These

Landing Chart for Manchester (CAA).

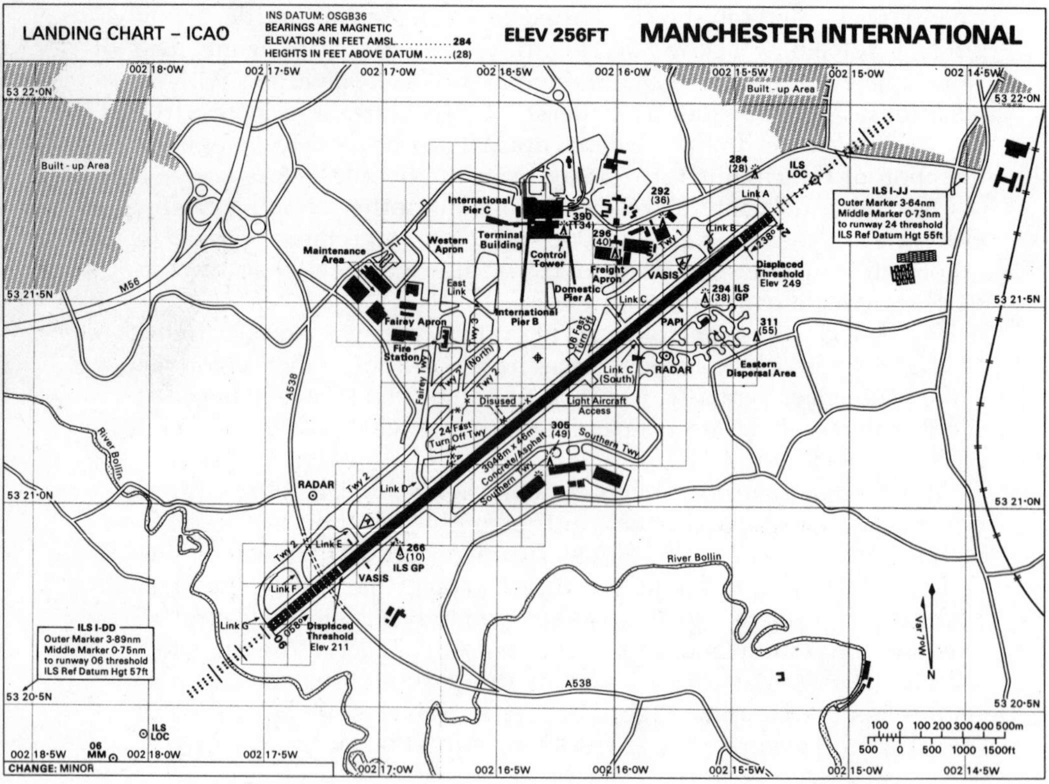

Approved Departure Times (ADTs) were formerly known as slot times and this terminology is still heard occasionally on R/T. Further details will be found below.

Certain domestic traffic within the United Kingdom, chiefly that inbound to airports in the London TMA, is also regulated at peak times. For example, from airports in the north of England a system known within ATC as 'DAVFLOW' applies, the word being derived from the Daventry Control Area in the Midlands. An aircraft from, say, Liverpool, will be required to cross the Honiley VOR south of Birmingham Airport within a specified time span of ten minutes. The term 'Honiley Slot' can thus be heard quite frequently.

If there are no problems, taxy instructions will be given to the appropriate runway. In the meantime, ATC will have obtained an airways clearance from the parent ATCC by land line and this is passed to the aircraft at a convenient moment. (Preferably not while

Landing Chart for Heathrow (CAA).

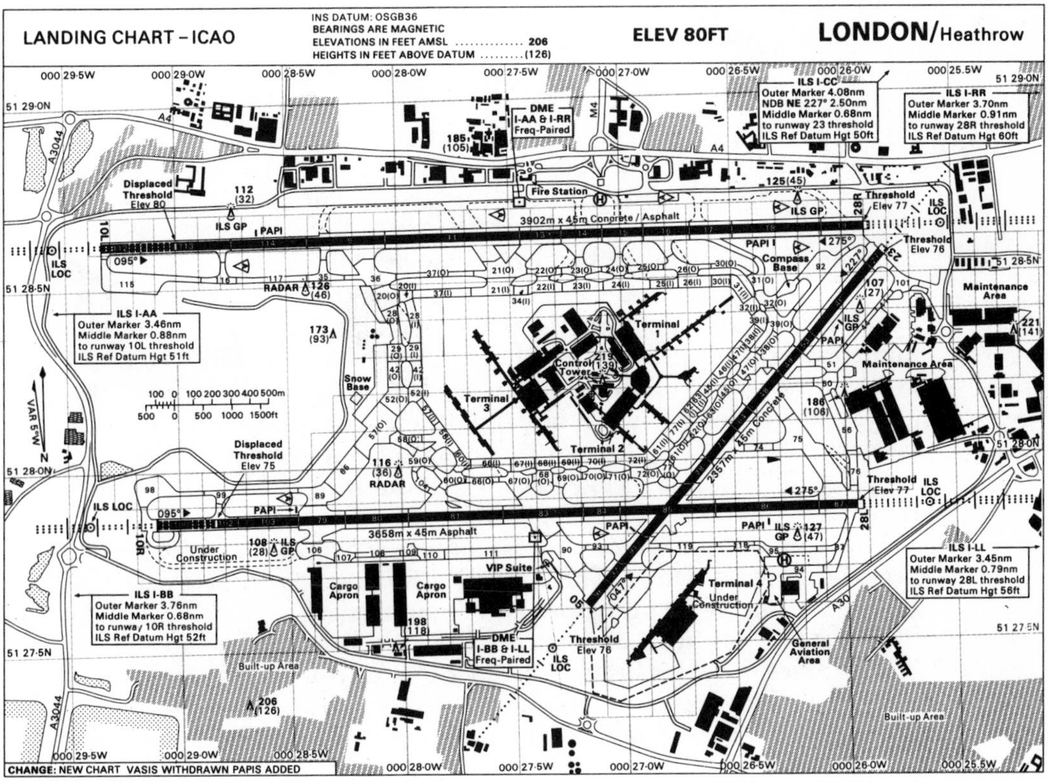

the crew are picking their way gingerly out of a crowded apron!) Local procedures vary from one airport to another and it may be necessary to contact the ATCC again as the subject nears the runway for permission to let it take off. Sometimes a restriction may be applied to separate it from overflying traffic, such as: 'Not above 2,500 ft until further cleared by Manchester Control.'

On occasion, the ATCC may allow the aircraft to take off with the condition that Approach Radar will separate it from inbound conflicting traffic. It will then be given a suitable radar heading to fly after departure and/or a level restriction. As soon as it is airborne the aircraft will be transferred to the Approach frequency and it will only be handed over to the ATCC when the confliction has been resolved.

Where no local restrictions are applied the Tower will put the aircraft over to the ATCC immediately after take-off. The departure time is also passed to the ATCC by telephone to be fed into the computer. At the busiest UK airports, including Heathrow, Gatwick and Manchester, the flow of arrivals and departures is designed so that the two do not conflict. The ideal is a 'conveyor belt' system but, although in practice this is virtually impossible to achieve, it comes quite near to being so. Of necessity the other lesser airfields in a TMA, for example Liverpool in the case of Manchester are somewhat subservient. Their traffic flows are very much subject to those of their busier neighbours, although on the credit side, sometimes more flexible.

Often, if the weather is good, pilots on IFR Flight plans may elect to go VFR. This saves en route navigational charges and it is also a way to avoid delays at busy periods when an airways clearance is not immediately forthcoming from the ATCC. However, pilots who try to beat the system and rejoin controlled airspace further down the airway will not get much sympathy! Public transport flights are not permitted to do this but cargo and mail pilots often make the request. A typical ATC acknowledgement of a request to go VFR is: 'WG919 roger, IFR flight plan cancelled at time 36.'

The SSR code or *squawk* as it is known, is allocated according to a predetermined system. The United Kingdom participates in the internationally agreed Originating Region Code Assignment Method (ORCAM). This was developed by Eurocontrol and endorsed by ICAO. Since there are insufficient code blocks to develop a world-wide system it has been necessary to group certain countries into Participating Areas. The ICAO EUR region is divided into five of these areas, the United Kingdom falling into PA West.

ORCAM is designed to reduce R/T and cockpit workload by allocating an SSR code which will be retained by the aircraft from take-off to touchdown. This helps controllers in forward planning, particularly in areas of radar data processing. Each ATCC is allocated two blocks of codes, one for internal flights (Domestic) and the other (ORCAM) for international flights. The ATCC with jurisdiction over the airspace first entered by an aircraft will assign a discrete code from one of its blocks. The code will depend on the destination and will be retained throughout the flight within the Participating Area, being transferred from centre to centre along the route.

Approach Control units with SSR capability have their own small block of codes which they can allocate to traffic crossing their area, provided of course that the aircraft is transponder-equipped. Fortunately nowadays most private aircraft can comply with this. Mention of the special *squawk* 4321 is often made on R/T. Pilots flying outside controlled airspace and Aerodrome Traffic Zones and who are not receiving a radar service are advised to set 4321, the conspicuity code, on the transponder. As the name implies, this makes the aircraft show up better on radar and the more sophisticated transponders will also indicate the altitude being maintained.

Aerodrome Control Phraseology

Aircraft: Luton Tower Britannia 835 request start-up.

ATC: Britannia 835 start-up approved, temperature plus 8.

These start-up requests should always be made by aircraft which intend to fly airways, as there may be unexpected delays. Far better to postpone starting for a few minutes than waste fuel at the holding point. The phrase 'Start-up at your discretion', together with an expected departure time, may be used so that the onus is on the crew to start engines at a convenient time. Note that the words 'at your discretion' are used by controllers to imply that any traffic delays, getting stuck in soft ground and similar misfortunes will henceforth be the pilot's fault! Controllers have very definite responsibilites and they are understandably reluctant to take on any extra ones.

Aircraft: London Ground Alitalia 235 Stand 28 request pushback.

ATC: Alitalia 235 pushback approved.

Many airports have nose-in parking at the terminal to save apron space and to facilitate passenger handling. Aircraft thus have to be pushed backwards by a tractor before they can taxy for departure.

Aircraft: Liverpool Tower GBDNR on the Western Apron request taxy for local.

Gatwick Visual Control Room with ASMI antenna on top (CAA).

ATC: GNR taxy to holding point runway 09 via Western Taxyway, QNH 1008.

Taxy instructions must always specify a clearance limit, which is the point at which an aircraft must halt and ask for further permission to proceed. The limit is normally the holding point of the runway in use but it may be an intermediate position, perhaps another runway which is also in intermittent use. To maintain a smooth operation, controllers try to anticipate calls from taxying aircraft so that they do not actually have to stop at intermediate points.

The ideal is to establish a circular flow of taxying aircraft so that the ones just landed do not get in the way of those moving towards the holding point. Alas, many airports have inadequate taxyway systems with two-way flows and bottlenecks, perhaps in the worst cases, as at Coventry, having runway access at only one end. A refusal to give crossing clearance of an active runway is given in the form: 'GVW hold short runway 23.' Permission to proceed is: 'GVW cross runway 23, report vacated.'

When ready for take-off, permission is sought from the Tower. If the runway is occupied by traffic which has just landed the aircraft will be told to 'line up'. The American phrase 'taxy into position' is sometimes tried when a foreign pilot seems to have difficulty in understanding what is meant. (Controllers always have something up their sleeves to break the language barrier and we have all had to resort to plain speech to convey our meaning to some uncomprehending student pilot!)

If there is traffic on final, the aircraft at the holding point may be told: 'After the Cherokee on short final, line up.' Care must be taken that there is no possibility of confusion with another aircraft which may have just landed. Where a preceding aircraft is beginning its take-off roll, the second aircraft may be told: 'After the departing F27, line up.' The use of the words 'cleared immediate take-off' means that the aircraft must go without delay to leave the runway free for landing traffic. It is only to be used where there is actual urgency so that its specific meaning is not debased.

I have already covered the circuit joining procedure, so a few examples of phraseology will suffice.

Aircraft: Coventry Tower GAYMN at Ansty for landing.

ATC: GMN join right hand downwind runway 05, QFE 1004; *or* GMN cleared straight-in approach runway 23, QFE 1004.

Aircraft: GMN downwind.

ATC: GMN Number 2, follow the Cessna 150 on base.

Aircraft: GMN Number 2, traffic in sight.

OR

ATC: GMN extend downwind, number 2 to a Cessna 150 4 miles final on radar approach.

Aircraft: GMN wilco.

Note that the obsolete standard phrase 'Cleared to final Number 2' etc may still be heard for some time as controllers under pressure occasionally revert to what they have been saying for the past decade or so. The word 'clear' or 'cleared' was swept away in the changes to R/T jargon in mid-1984 and is now reserved solely for landing, take-off and route clearances in order to reduce dangerous misunderstandings.

Having already explained the criteria for issuing landing and take-off clearances, it only remains for me to mention a few extra points. Aircraft on what used to be known as 'circuits and bumps' may wish to do a 'touch and go' landing; in other words, the aircraft lands, continues rolling and takes off again without a pause. The wording 'cleared touch and go' is the only one approved officially but pilots may ask for a 'roller', the military equivalent.

Instructions to carry out a missed approach may be given to avert an unsafe situation, such as when one aircraft is too close behind another on final. 'GTE go around, I say again, go around. Acknowledge.' However, it is likely that the phrase which this replaced in 1984, 'Overshoot, I say again overshoot. Acknowledge' will still be with us for a while, so deeply has it penetrated pilots' and controllers' consciousness.

Depending on local procedures, a departing aircraft will be retained on the Tower frequency until it is clear of the area or changed to

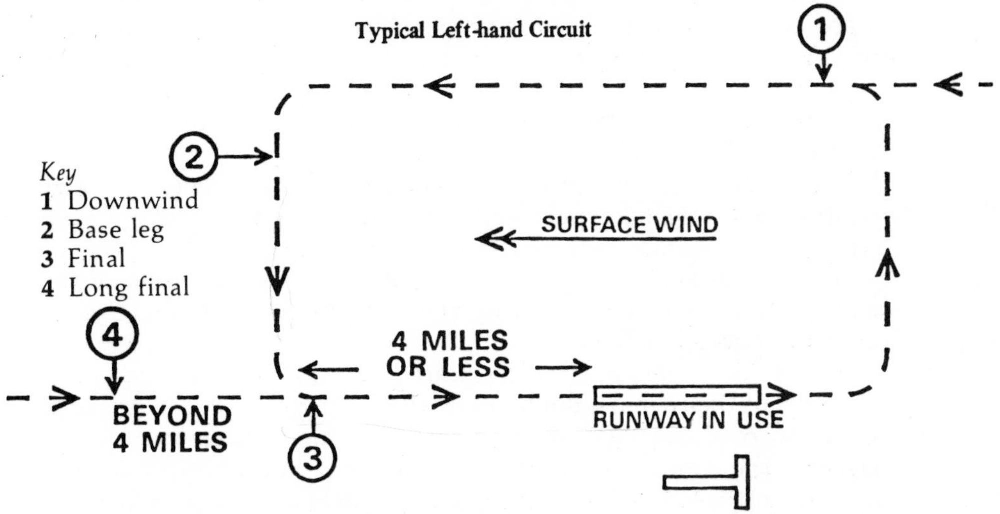

Above *Critical positions in the Traffic Circuit.*

Left *Night scene in the Tower at Manchester* (CAA).

Below *Taxyway and stand designations for Stansted* (CAA).

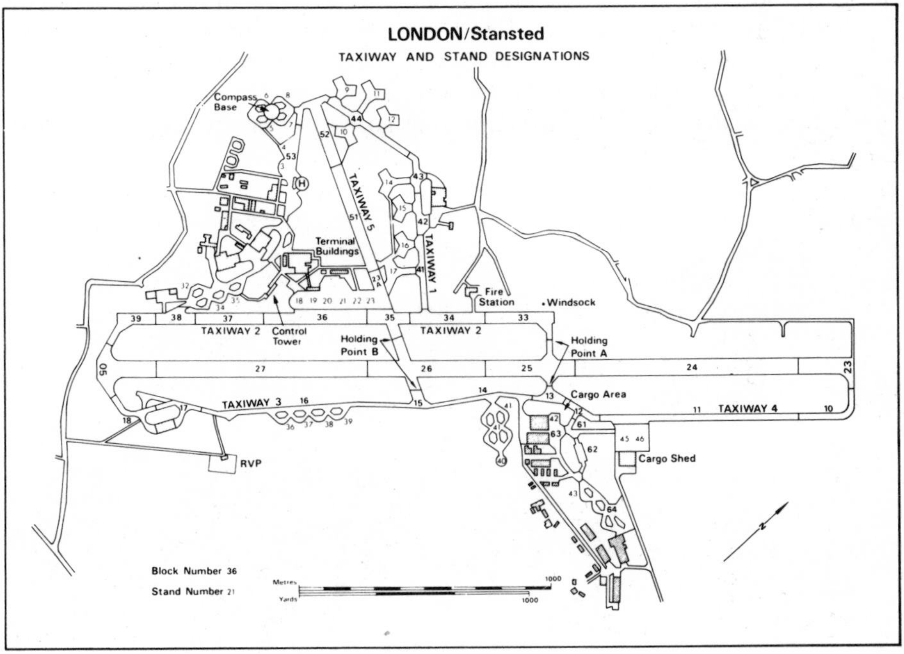

Approach immediately. Airways flights will of course be transferred to the ATCC just after take-off or as soon as they have been separated from any conflicting traffic. When the landing roll is complete, the arriving aircraft will be told to clear the runway in the following manner:

ATC: GMN vacate left; *or* GMN taxi to the end, report runway vacated; *or* GMN take next right. When vacated contact Ground 118.35.

The appropriate taxying instructions are then passed. Airborne and landing times may be passed by the Tower, although there is no official requirement for this.

Interestingly enough, controllers are not responsible for reminding pilots to put their wheels down on final, except when a radar approach is being provided. However, if an aircraft landed wheels-up in broad daylight, the controller would no doubt come in for some criticism, apart from the dent to his professional pride! Fortunately it is a rare occurrence these days but I once earned a pint from a Cessna 337 pilot whom I reminded just in time. (Cheap at the price—the saving in repairs would have paid my year's salary!)

One last point is defined as 'Essential Aerodrome Information' and refers to any obstruction or unserviceability which is likely to affect operations. It is always prefixed 'caution' and some examples follow:

Caution work in progress ahead north side of the taxyway.

Caution VASIs runway 27 unserviceable.

Caution large flock of birds north of runway 27 near the fast turn off.

Chapter 8

ATC at Heathrow

Because of its intensity, Heathrow traffic is handled rather differently from that of other British airports, hence a separate chapter to explain the methods. Inbound aircraft are directed by LATCC to one of four VORs located at Bovingdon, Lambourne, Biggin and Ockham. If traffic is light they may not actually route overhead these beacons but are vectored by radar directly to intercept the ILS for the runway in use. As the traffic flow increases, aircraft may arrive at the beacons faster than the airport is able to receive them, allowing for the requisite separation on approach. Hence the term 'stacking' (in ATC more usually referred to as 'holding'). The aircraft fly an oval racetrack pattern aligned in a specified direction. The outbound leg from the beacon is flown for one minute, then a rate one turn (a change of direction of 3° per second) onto a one minute inbound leg, finally a further rate one turn to the beacon, and so on.

During Heathrow's busy periods six controllers work as a team. They consist of two Approach Controllers, two Number One Radar Controllers, a Number Two Radar Controller and a Special VFR Controller. Each Approach Controller with his Number One radar man controls the traffic from either Bovingdon and Lambourne in the north or from Ockham and Biggin in the south. As the aircraft nears the reporting point LATCC releases it to Heathrow Approach on intercom as pre-warning that it is about to call. On contact the pilot is told to enter the hold or, if there is no delay, vectored directly into the landing sequence.

The Approach Controllers and the Number One Radar Controllers work closely together, instructing pilots to adjust their height, speed and heading so that two orderly streams of aircraft, one from the north, the other from the south are brought onto the approach path. Aircraft in these two streams are handed over to the Number Two Radar Controller so that he can integrate them into a single stream of aircraft approaching the runway.

At this stage a correct landing interval must be established and the Number Two Radar Controller ensures that all aircraft are correctly separated, depending on the prevailing weather conditions and type of

Opposite *Radar display for the London TMA at a busy time. Callsign and height information is shown, together with codes for destinations eg KK for Gatwick and LL for Heathrow* (CAA).

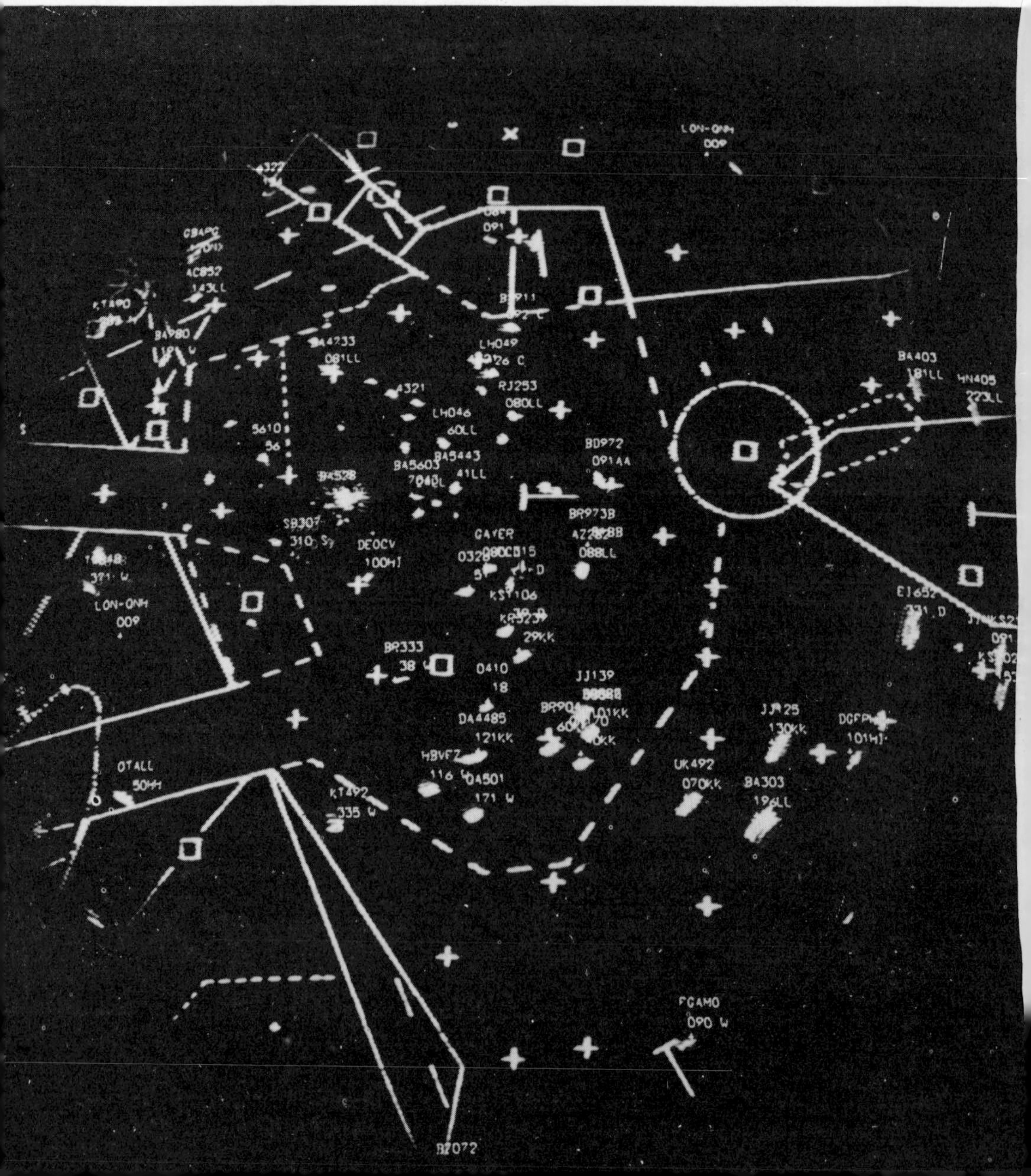

aircraft involved. The vortex wake separations are explained in Chapter 13 but there are other considerations. For example, a DC-9 following a Shorts 360 will obviously have no problem with vortex wake but will catch up rapidly if this is not allowed for. Similarly, if visibility is on limits an aircraft may be slow to clear the runway and the 'land after' procedure cannot be applied, resulting in an overshoot if the next aircraft is too close behind.

The Special VFR Controller is responsible for helicopters and light aircraft which want to land or merely transit the London Control Zone within the levels for which Heathrow Approach is responsible. Inbound aircraft are fitted into the approach pattern to cause as little inconvenience as possible to the main commercial traffic. Helicopters are required to follow special routes in the London area, designed where possible to keep them over the River Thames and the most thinly populated areas.

The usual destination is the Westland Heliport at Battersea. All inbound helicopters have to route via the River Thames, initially positioning to Kew Bridge, Barnes or London Bridge, depending upon the direction from which they are approaching. There are numerous compulsory and on request reporting points and helicopters may be held at a number of positions to await onward clearance. They are all located at easily recognizable places such as Hampton Court, Sunbury Lock, and Hanworth.

When the two streams of approaching aircraft are satisfactorily merged into one, and as each aircraft is established on the ILS at a distance of six to eight miles from touchdown, control is transferred to Air Arrivals Control in the Tower. Like any other Tower Controller he issues landing clearances, and passes wind checks and details of surface conditions where appropriate.

After the aircraft has landed and left the runway it will be transferred to the Ground Movements Controller who directs it to the parking stand. He continues to monitor its progress and co-ordinates its movements with those of other aircraft and vehicles. Any airport has its quota of service vehicles but Heathrow inevitably has more than most. There is, for example, a full time mobile bird control unit to deter the large flocks which stray from the reservoirs bordering the airport.

The maintenance of runways and taxyways and their associated lighting is one of the biggest problems for Ground Movement Control. One controller told me that there is almost always some part of the airport being dug up or resurfaced. Each controller has an

ARRIVALS via LAMBOURNE LONDON/Heathrow

GENERAL INFORMATION
1 Standard routes may be varied at the discretion of ATC.
2 Cross Speed Limit Points (SLP) or 3min before holding facility at 250kts IAS or less.
3 Due to proximity of Danger Area EG D138 do not fly south of track Abeam **CLN VOR** until **BRAINTREE SOUTH**.
4 When Danger Area EG D144 is active the route will be : **REFSO-BLUSY-LONGSAND-TRIPO-LAM**
5 When **LAM VOR** is out of service aircraft approaching from East will proceed on **TAWNY**.
6 As lowest level in **LAM/TAWNY** holding stacks (7000') is above transition altitude, aircraft will be instructed by ATC to fly at the appropriate flight level.

NOT TO SCALE

TRANSITION LEV ATC
TRANS ALT 6000'

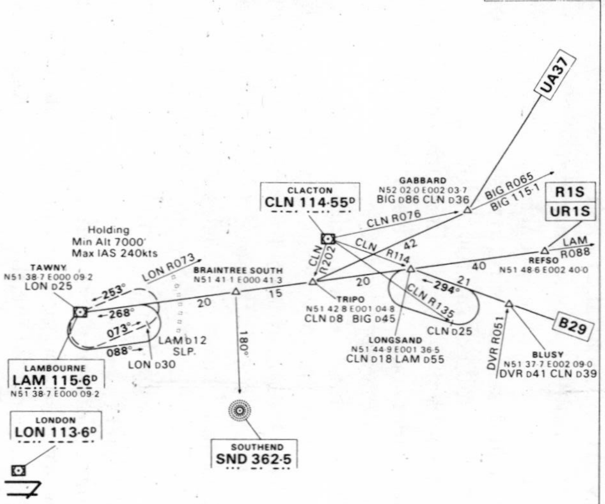

Standard Terminal Arrival Chart for Heathrow (CAA).

CHANGE BEARINGS, RADIALS.

AERO INF DATE 18 Nov 86

ARRIVALS via OCKHAM LONDON/ Heathrow

GENERAL INFORMATION
1 Standard routes may be varied at the discretion of ATC.
2 Cross Speed Limit Points (SLP) or 3min before holding facility at 250kts IAS or less.
3 When **OCK VOR** is out of service hold on **EPM NDB**. If instructed to hold at 3000' inbound track will be 274°M turning left at **EPM NDB**.
4 As lowest level in **OCK/EPM** holding stacks (7000') is above transition altitude, aircraft will be instructed by ATC to fly at the appropriate flight level.

NOT TO SCALE

TRANSITION LEV ATC
TRANS ALT 6000'

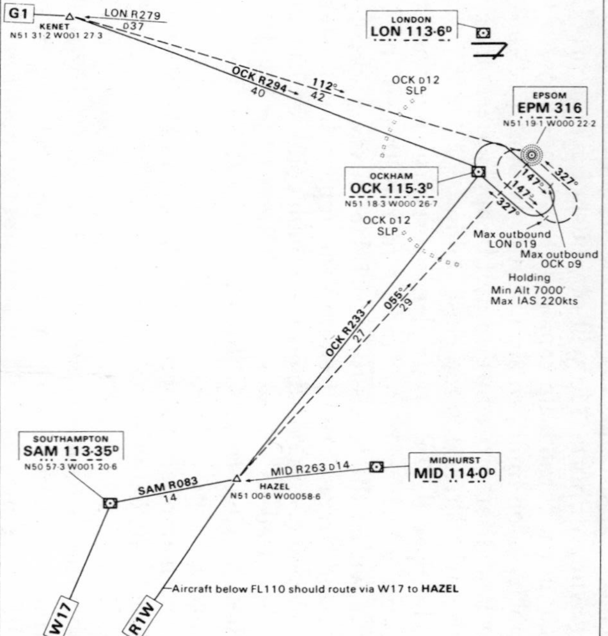

CHANGE BEARINGS, RADIALS.

AERO INF DATE 18 Nov 86

airport plan on which he notes the current unserviceable areas before taking over watch in the Tower. For easy reference Heathrow is divided up into numbered blocks.

To help things run smoothly at night or in poor visibility a radar called the Aerodrome Surface Movement Indicator (ASMI) is used to monitor aircraft and vehicle movements. Its aerial is mounted on top of the Tower and scans the airport at very high speed so that the radar picture is continuously renewed. Runways and taxyways show up clearly on the display, as do the aircraft and vehicles which need to be tracked. Like television, it is bright enough for daylight viewing.

At night the aircraft are assisted by green centreline and red stop bar lights set flush with the taxyway. These can be illuminated in sections to allow a discrete route to be signalled to ensure that no two aircraft are in or crossing the same section at any one time. This complex lighting system is operated by an ATC assistant on instructions from the Ground Movements Controller. The lighting control panel is a mimic diagram, ie it is designed in the form of an airport plan with switches which directly operate the lighting in the corresponding section on the airport.

When an aircraft is ready for departure, the pilot calls the Ground Movement Planner for permission to start engines. This may be granted at once or a start time given to minimise ground delays and thus save fuel. Also taken into consideration are the number of other aircraft which have started up, air route congestion and ADTs issued by LATCC.

Once start-up clearance is given the pilot is told to contact GMC when ready to taxy. The latter is responsible for issuing push-back clearance from the stand by a tractor. Guidance is then given to the runway in use, and as this is approached, the aircraft is handed over to the Air Departures Controller who arranges the aircraft in a departure sequence to achieve the maximum use of the runway concerned.

For example, when two aircraft of a similar type are departing in succession, one for a north bound destination followed by one to the south, they may be allowed to leave one minute apart. However, due to the variety of aircraft types using Heathrow, this time interval may be increased depending on aircraft type and specific departure route. Immediately it is airborne the aircraft is transferred to London Control and fitted into the airways system.

Chapter 9

Oceanic Control

Although traffic over the North Atlantic communicates with ATC by means of the HF radio band, VHF being too restricted in range, aircraft requesting clearance to enter the Shanwick Oceanic Control Area from overhead the United Kingdom can be heard on certain VHF frequencies. ATC in the Shanwick OCA is provided by the Oceanic ATCC at Prestwick, supported by the communications station at Ballygireen near Shannon in Eire, hence the composite callsign Shanwick Oceanic. Jet aircraft are required to request oceanic clearance while east of 2°W or as early as possible if departing from a point west of 2°W, so it is easy to intercept their transmissions in much of the United Kingdom.

For sub-sonic aircraft over the Atlantic there is a procedure known as the organised track system. As a result of passenger demands, time zone differences and airport noise restrictions, much of the North Atlantic air traffic is contained in two flows—westbound in the morning and eastbound in the evening. Because of the concentration of the flows and the limited vertical height band which is economical for jet operations, the airspace is comparatively congested. The track system is thus designed to accommodate as many aircraft as possible on the most suitable flight paths, taking advantage of any pressure systems to provide a tail wind where possible.

Prestwick OACC is responsible for the day track system and Gander for that at night. In each case, planners on both sides of the Atlantic consult with one another and co-ordinate as necessary with adjacent OACCs, as well as with domestic ATC agencies, to ensure that the system provides sufficient tracks and Flight Levels to satisfy anticipated traffic demands.

On completion of negotiations the organised tracks system is sent out by the OACC concerned by signal to all interested parties in Europe and North America. The daytime system is usually published by Prestwick between midnight and 01:00 hours. Gander usually publishes its night system between noon and 13:00 hours. In addition, the track co-ordinates are broadcast on frequency 133.8 and this can be heard in many parts of the United Kingdom on a normal air band radio. The tracks are known as Alfa, Bravo, Charlie and so on, the most northerly being Alfa.

Each oceanic flight plan received from the departure airport includes the track, Flight Level and cruise Mach number requested. (Mach number being a proportion of Mach 1, the speed of sound.) When the pilot requests an oceanic clearance, the Planning Controller attempts to fit the flight into the planned slot according to the aircraft's requested level, Mach number and boundary estimate.

Once the clearance is accepted by the pilot, the information is relayed to the relevant ATCC and, where necessary, to adjacent OACCs. Then the clearance is fed into Prestwick's computer which prints the appropriate en route flight strips and passes the information to Gander's computer. This flight strip gives all relevant flight details and computed times of arrival at specific reporting points along the track, normally at intervals of 10° of longitude. This flight strip is used by the controller to monitor the progress of the flight through the OCA.

Compared with the brief content of domestic airways clearances, these oceanic clearances are fairly long-winded because of the need to specify a large number of latitude and longitude positions, although in certain circumstances they can be abbreviated. It is useful to record these messages on tape for subsequent analysis, the same going for other ATC transmissions when you are using an air band radio for the first time.

Most flights across the North Atlantic are handled in this way, but some aircraft may wish to operate outside the organised track system, for example on flights between Europe and the Caribbean, or between Europe and the West Coast of the USA. These too are handled by Shanwick, as are transatlantic flights by Concorde. The latter operate along fixed tracks, normally between 50,000 ft and 60,000 ft. Because of the extremely small number of aircraft flying within this height band it is usually possible for the OACC to issue a clearance before take-off. This allows Concorde to operate on a supersonic 'cruise climb profile', which is the best in terms of fuel economy.

Unique to oceanic control is the method by which aircraft request clearances. Irrespective of geographical location, an aircraft will always use one of two frequencies, either 123.95 or 127.65 mhz.

Aircraft registered west of 30°W use the first one, those registered east of 30°W the second. In practice this generally means that British airlines use 127.65 and American, Australian and Canadian airlines use 123.95.

Over most of the North Atlantic the airspace between 27,500 ft and 40,000 ft is known as MNPS (Minimum Navigation Performance Specification) airspace. Aircraft flying within it are required to carry a certain scale of navigation equipment so that they can be flown accurately within the parameters of the clearance. In this congested airspace any deviation could be dangerous.

HF radio is used for trans-oceanic flights because of its long range. This is outside the scope of this book but occasional mention of Selcal codes within the clearance refers to the Selective Calling System. So that the crew does not have to monitor the radio continuously during a long flight, a coded radio signal is transmitted to the aircraft. Each flight has its own individual code and on receipt by the aircraft's decoder, Selcal operates a flashing light and/or a chime signal in the cockpit. The crew thus alerted will then reply to the ground in the normal way.

Concorde flying over the Atlantic is a special case because an idealised flight profile would commence with an uninterrupted climb to supersonic cruise, followed by an uninterrupted descent to destination. Sonic boom considerations and the presence of other traffic obviously render this impossible so, in order to avoid supersonic flight over the UK land mass, a typical flight to the USA via the Woodley and Lyneham beacons climbs initially to around FL 260 and maintains Mach .95 until the 'nominal acceleration point' after crossing the coastline south of Brecon. The final tactical consideration for clearance for transonic acceleration along the Bristol Channel is made by the Radar Controller at LATCC. Likewise, on the return trip the transonic deceleration is completed over the sea prior to crossing the coast.

Concorde has special, unvarying oceanic tracks, known as 'Sierra Mike' when westbound and 'Sierra November' or 'Sierra Oscar' when eastbound.

Air France Concorde flights to North America depart from Paris Charles de Gaulle and enter the London UIR south-west of Lands End. They then route to the same oceanic entry point at 50°N 08°W.

Chapter 10

Flight Information Services

An ATC service can be provided only by licensed controllers but at certain small airfields an Aerodrome Flight Information Service (AFIS) is in operation. The AFIS Officers, AFISOs for short, are also required to be licensed and many of them are flying instructors doing this ground job on a part-time basis. Air band listeners will notice certain differences in the R/T phraseology used by AFISOs, reflecting the fact that their instructions are of an advisory nature only. For example, where a licensed controller would say 'cleared take-off', an AFISO would say 'take off at your discretion.'

The aerodrome air/ground service (A/G) is a rudimentary one, for which no qualifications are required, although persons providing it must possess an 'Authority to Operate.' It is usually encountered at private aerodromes used by perhaps one or two company aircraft, Wrexham in North Wales and Tatenhill in Staffordshire being examples. Basic information is passed to the pilots, covering such essentials as the wind direction and whether the runway is clear. The callsigns for AFIS and A/G are 'INFORMATION' and 'RADIO', respectively.

The Flight Information Service provided by licensed controllers at ATCCs on a 24-hour basis is somewhat different and requires further explanation. The London FIR outside controlled airspace is divided into three, west and east of Amber 1 and north of Blue 1, with separate radio frequencies. For the Scottish FIR, one is considered sufficient because of the lighter traffic.

The FIR controller is able to offer the following services; weather information, changes of serviceability of radio navigation aids, aerodrome conditions, proximity warnings and any other information pertinent to safety. Because of the multiplicity of possible reporting points in the FIR, ranging from disused airfields to towns and coastal features, it is difficult to assess the possibility of collision and therefore no positive control or separation can be provided. The other problem is that of civil and military aircraft on random tracks and for whom there is no requirement to contact the FIR.

Outside controlled airspace, a Radar Advisory Service is provided by certain ATC units, subject to the coverage of the radar equipment and the unit's workload. Where such a service is given by an airfield approach unit, it is usually limited to a range of 40 km from the aerodrome traffic zone. Pilots are informed of the bearing, distance, and, if available, the level of the conflicting traffic with advice on the action to be taken to maintain separation if the pilot does not have the traffic in sight. If the pilot decides to ignore the advice given, whether he has visual contact or not, he is responsible for any avoiding action that may subsequently prove necessary.

An alternative is the Radar Information Service, in which the participating pilot is warned of conflicting traffic. No avoiding action is offered and the pilot is wholly responsible for maintaining separation from other aircraft, whether or not the controller has passed traffic information. A pilot wishing to take advantage of an RAS or RIS must first establish verbal agreement with the controller, no radar service being provided until this agreement has been reached. A request for an RAS to be upgraded to an RIS will be accepted subject to the controller's existing workload.

Since mid-1983, military ATC radar units have been providing a Lower Airspace Radar Advisory Service (LARS) to any aircraft outside controlled airspace which requests it. The upper limit is, with certain exceptions, FL 95, and the service is given within about 30 miles of each participating unit. Overlapping coverage ensures that Eastern England and the Midlands and South are well-served, but over Wales and the North-West there are only Brawdy, Valley and Shawbury. Whenever possible aircraft will be handed over from one controller to the next and pilots told to contact the next unit.

Chapter 11

Weather and Air Traffic Control

Met observations at the larger airports are made every 30 minutes at 20 minutes past and 10 minutes to each hour. At the less busy airports they are made once in each hour. Special observations, known as SPECIs (pronounced 'Spessys') must be made within these times if certain changes are observed, eg at the onset or cessation of hail or thunderstorms. If there is a Met Office available, the observations will be done by met staff who are all employees of the Ministry of Defence. Otherwise they are made by ATC personnel who are required to hold a Met Observer's Certificate, gained after a short course at the Met College.

There is a standard format which is passed to the aircraft, consisting of the wind direction in degrees True and its average speed in knots with a note of any significant gusts. This is, however, normally read by the controller in degrees Magnetic direct from the dial in front of him so that it can be related by the pilot to the magnetic heading of the runway. The visibility is passed in metres and kilometres in increments of 100 m when 5,000 m or less and in whole kilometres when greater than 5,000 m. The distance is determined from the known ranges of conspicuous landmarks visible in the locality. The next item is the weather, eg drizzle, fog, rain and so on.

Cloud base is measured by means of a cloud base recorder which scans the sky overhead with a laser beam. Unfortunately, it may give inaccurate low readings when haze, mist or smoke is present. At less well-equipped airfields, cloud base is found by estimation, with experience a surprisingly accurate method. Pilot reports can be requested to confirm the base. At night estimation is difficult so a vertical searchlight is often used. The angle of the 'spot' on the cloud can then be found by sighting with a simple instrument known as an alidade. Simple pre-calculated trigonometry enables the cloud height to be read off a table.

A third method, a small hydrogen or helium-filled balloon of about 2 ft diameter, can be used to measure a lowish base in daylight. The balloon rises at a known rate and can thus be timed with a stop-watch until it disappears into the cloud. It is, however, time-consuming and necessitates heavy, and in the case of hydrogen, highly inflammable, gas cylinders being stored adjacent to the Tower, so few airfields still use it today.

Cloud amount is given in oktas, ie eighths, and height in feet up to and including 5,000 ft. Cloud above this level is of academic interest only to aircrew so is not reported. Not more than three layers are reported, the exception being when cumulo-nimbus cloud, known as Cb or Charlie Bravo, is present. If necessary this can be reported as a fourth group with some emphasis as its turbulence and lightning discharges are an obvious hazard to aircraft.

Air temperature is passed in degrees Celsius, together with the dew point if the two figures are significantly close, indicating that fog may be about to form. The QNH and QFE (Threshold QFE at certain airfields) is given in millibars. These units may one day become hectopascals in the United Kingdom and are already referred to as such in certain European ATC systems. American aircraft occasionally ask for the pressure settings in inches of mercury so a table is kept handy in the Tower for a quick conversion.

Where the weather conditions meet particular criteria—visibility of 10 km or more, no precipitation, no thunderstorm or shallow fog, no cloud below a level of 5,000 ft above aerodrome elevation and no Cb at any level—the visibility and cloud groups are omitted and the word 'CAVOK' (pronounced 'cav OK') is passed. This is derived from the phrase Ceiling and Visibility OK but it seems to confuse a lot of private pilots!

At the busiest UK airports the current met observation is transmitted continuously on the appropriate Terminal VOR frequency by means of a pre-recorded tape. A transcript of a typical broadcast for Birmingham on the Honiley VOR is as follows: 'This is Birmingham Arrival Information Juliet. 13:20 weather, 300 at 15 knots, 8 kilometres recent rain, 7 okta 1,500 ft, temperature plus 8, dew point plus 7, QNH 1001 millibars. Landing runway 33. Report Information Juliet received on first contact with Birmingham Approach.'

The significance of Juliet is that each observation is given a code letter, beginning with Alfa and working through the alphabet, starting once more when Zulu is reached. The controller is thus sure that the pilot has copied the latest observation. In addition, Heathrow has a similar broadcast on a different frequency for departing aircraft, using the prefix 'Heathrow Departure Information'. These automatic transmissions are very useful in reducing R/T loading as crews can monitor them at their leisure and the controller does not have to pass repeated weather information. It will be noted that the QFE is not included in the ATIS broadcast (Automatic Terminal Information Service). Because of its vital importance this is left to Approach Control to pass.

Runway Visual Range, or RVR as it normally referred to, makes available a more localised assessment of how far the pilot is likely to be able to see along the runway. Measurement only begins when the official met report gives a general visibility of 1,500 m or less and it is essential to enable the pilot to decide whether or not it is within the limits of what are known as 'company minima' for landing or take-off.

RVR is calculated by either the human observer method or by means of electronic equipment. The former requires a person, usually an airport fireman, to stand on a vehicle adjacent to the runway threshold at a specified height to simulate pilot eye-level. He then counts the number of lights or, at some locations, marker boards, that he can see down one side of the runway. The total is passed by radio to the Tower and the RVR read off a pre-computed table.

The Instrumented RVR system, called IRVR, measures the opacity of the atmosphere and gives a constant read-out in the Tower of the RVR at three fixed points on the runway, referred to as touchdown, mid-point and stop end, and can easily be switched manually to the opposite end if required.

The term *sigmet* is sometimes heard on R/T, this being a warning of such hazardous phenomena as thunderstorms, severe turbulence and severe airframe icing. Another jargon word is *nosig*, short for no significant change, and sometimes appended to aerodrome forecasts when passed on the radio. The term *trend* is employed to indicate the way the weather is likely to go, codes like *tempo* for a temporary change being added as appropriate.

A hazard which has always been with us but has only recently become recognised is that of wind shear. In the last seven years there have been at least a dozen serious accidents to large airliners directly attributable to wind shear and pilots can often be heard reporting its presence on final approach to the Tower so that following aircraft can be warned.

Briefly, wind shear is a change of windspeed and/or direction between two points in the atmosphere. By such a definition it is almost always present and normally does not cause undue difficulty to the pilot. However, on take-off or landing what amounts to an instantaneous change in headwind can be dangerous. An instantaneous decrease in headwind on the approach will tend to increase the rate of descent and an instantaneous increase in headwind will tend to decrease it. In both cases the pilot is faced with a rapid change in airspeed, coupled with a departure from the glide path and either a 'hot and long' or a short landing become likely.

Horizontal wind shears are generally outflows from the bases of Cb clouds or are caused by the passage of active weather fronts. Local topographical features, both natural and artificial, can also cause shear. Buildings and other large structures close to runways can spark off turbulence and rotor effects, with marked differences in wind direction. Since wind shear is obviously invisible, much experimental work is being carried out with acoustic Dopplers, Doppler radar and optical lasers to try to detect and measure it. Heathrow is unique in the United Kingdom in having a wind shear alerting service. Certain weather criteria are used to assess its possible presence and this is backed up by pilot reports. The alert message is inserted in the arrival and departure ATIS broadcasts.

Another major hazard to aircraft is fortunately easier to measure. This is braking action when the runway is icy, or if snow or slush is present. There are two methods of determining it; the simple Tapley Meter decelerometer and the sophisticated (and expensive) device which has largely superseded it, the Mu Meter. The latter consists of a runway friction measuring trailer towed by a vehicle travelling at 40 mph. It provides an automatic print-out of the mean co-efficient of friction at three equi-distant points along the runway. When manual mode is selected, further readings can be obtained as required. The lower the figure the worse the braking action, eg something like 0.25 would indicate a very icy surface, 0.85 would be a dry runway.

The word *snowtam* refers to an ingenious system of describing and tabulating runway conditions under snow, slush or ice and the degree to which they are cleared or about to be cleared. Braking action as determined above is also included. A series of letters and figures, each referring to a specific detail, can easily be decoded on receipt by telex.

Finally, in many parts of the country it is possible to pick up the broadcasts of the London Volmet Service, the Vol part of the title being derived from the French word for flight. Weather conditions in a standardised form are transmitted continuously for the main UK and selected European airports. Pilots can thus monitor Volmet whilst en route and note the current conditions at their destination and suitable alternatives without having to make specific calls for the information. If their destination is a smaller airfield not on the Volmet they can either call it direct or request the information via London or Scottish Flight Information who will obtain it by telephone.

There are three separate broadcasts on different VHF frequencies:
London Volmet North—126.6 Mhz;
London Volmet South—128.6;
London Volmet Main—135.375.

Volmet North is sent out from Great Dun Fell in Cumbria, South and Main are both transmitted simultaneously from Davidstow Moor in Cornwall, Ventnor, Isle of Wight and Warlingham, south of London. The rather mechanical speech is due to the fact that the message is made up from a store of individual words and short phrases on tape, which are selected by a computer and then joined to form the required sentences.

The presentation of the information is as described above but where significant changes are expected, one of the following will be heard:

Gradu The change is expected at a constant rate.

Rapid The change is expected in a short period of less than 30 minutes.

Tempo The change is expected to last for less than one hour.

Inter Frequent changes are expected, fluctuating almost constantly.

Trend A change is anticipated but it is expected to occur slowly throughout the period.

London Volmet Main broadcasts the half-hourly reports for Heathrow, Gatwick, Birmingham, Manchester, Prestwick, Dublin, Amsterdam, Brussels, and Paris/Charles de Gaulle. London Volmet South is responsible for Heathrow, Gatwick, Luton, Bournemouth, Stansted, East Midlands, Southend, Cardiff and Jersey. London Volmet North transmits those for Heathrow, Manchester, Glasgow, Edinburgh, Prestwick, Aldergrove, Aberdeen, Newcastle and Leeds.

Chapter 12

Airfield visual aids

Airfield lighting ranges from the rudimentary edge lights found at many smaller locations to the complex and impressive systems to be seen at major airports. The paraffin flares from an earlier era, known as 'goosenecks', are still in use at a few places as emergency lighting, but are gradually being replaced by portable battery lamps which are easier to handle but no more effective.

On certain instrument runways the caution zone, ie the last 600 m, may have yellow rather than white lights. In addition the centreline is usually delineated by flush-fitting lights for the whole length. These are colour-coded to give an indication of the distance remaining in poor visibility. The lights are coloured red over the final 300 m and alternately red and white between 900 m and 300 m from the runway end.

As well as centreline lighting, all runways which comply with Precision Approach Category 2 and 3 lighting standard are provided with Touchdown Zone lights (TDZs). These consist of many flush-fitting white lights set into each side of the centreline in the first 900 m of the runway. A row of green threshold lights marks the beginning of the paved surface and a similar line of red ones marks the stop end.

Approach lighting is usually non-existent at small aerodromes and at others varies in standard, depending upon the approach aids and type of traffic handled. The approach lights at major airports begin at an average distance of 300 m out from the threshold and extend for a further 900 m out on the approach. They consist of a centreline and up to five cross-bars in white lights. Where Category 2 and 3 lighting standard is required, red supplementary approach lighting is provided within the basic system for the inner 300 m as an extra aid for landing in marginal weather conditions. All lighting is controlled in intensity from the Tower, the criteria being laid down clearly for differing met conditions.

The lights are displayed all the time at busy airports but the normal requirement for them to be on in daylight hours is whenever the visibility is less than six kilometres and/or the cloud base less than 700 ft. At night when traffic is light at some places, the lights are turned on 15 minutes before an ETA and left on until 15 minutes after an aircraft has departed.

Taxyway lights are standardised as green for the centreline and blue for the edges. The latter are used only to delineate apron edges and as an extra guide for bends in taxyways. The lights are 15 m apart which is reduced to 7½ m for Category 3 systems. Red stop bars mark holding points, especially those at runway entrances. There may also be traffic lights for airfield vehicles. Both can be operated from the Tower and the stop bars normally have a short time delay so that they revert to red after an aircraft has passed. London Heathrow has a particularly elaborate system of lighting for the control of taxyways.

Fast turn-offs, or rapid exit taxyways as they are coming to be known, only have their centreline lights lit from the runway direction. The lights in the opposite direction are now required to be blanked off to prevent inadvertent infringement of an active runway. This was yet another result of the enquiry into the Teneriffe collision.

Runway guard lights, consisting of a pair of alternately flashing lights and known colloquially as 'wig-wags', may be located at either side of holding positions. The purpose of these yellow lights is to improve the conspicuity of holding points and to warn pilots of the proximity of an active runway.

Once a pilot on approach is within sight of the runway, visual guidance is provided by Visual Approach Slope Indicators (VASIS). They show lights of two colours and are arranged to form two pairs of white/red wingbars extending each side of the runway and are generally located at 300 m and 1,500 m up the runway from the threshold. The indications given are:

All bars white—high approach
Near bars white, far bars red—normal approach
All bars red—low approach

The normal VASI system may not provide sufficient wheel clearance over the threshold for very large aircraft due to the difference in height between the pilot's eye level and the landing gear. To meet this problem the three-bar VASI is installed at airports regularly used by such aircraft. A third pair of wing bars is sited further along the runway to form another approach channel above the normal one.

Fast replacing VASI units is the Precision Approach Path Indicator—PAPI for short. This is smaller, easier to maintain, uses less power than VASI and gives better information to the pilot. Four PAPI lights are placed in line to the left of the runway threshold. They are arranged so that when the pilot is on the approach path two appear white and the other two are red. When a third light shows red, the pilot knows he is getting slightly low, when all four are red he is significantly below the glide path. Conversely, four white indications tell him he is too high.

From the pilot's point of view, PAPI gives crisper indications and is usable right down to touchdown—VASI cannot be used below 200 ft. PAPI is effective out to a range of about 20 km, compared with about 5 km for VASI. It also performs better when the pilot is looking into bright sunlight.

A number of the smaller airfields have an installation called LITAS (Low Intensity Two Colour Slope System). It is basically similar to VASI but has lights of lower intensity placed generally on the left hand side of the runway only. Interpretation of the information is identical to that for VASI and, although designed for use at night, the system has been found to give assistance by day in anything other than bright sunlight.

The other major visual aids on airports are the painted markings on the manoeuvring area. All runways in regular use will have centreline and threshold markings, the latter varying from the designator number alone to separate 'piano keys' and designator, depending upon the importance of the runway and its associated instrument aids. Whilst threshold markings are usually at the end of the runway, they sometimes need to be displaced upwind if, for example, there are obstacles like a public road on the approach. Arrows then indicate that the first portion of the runway is sterile for landing.

All runways more than 1,600 m long without VASI or PAPI, and all precision instrument runways, will have an additional symbol 300 m from the landing threshold known as the 'fixed distance marker'. The apparent distance between this and the threshold marking, seen from the approach, should aid pilots in judging their angle of descent and the two markings also bracket the optimum Touchdown Zone on the runway.

Touchdown Zone markings, extending for a distance of at least 600 m from the threshold, will be provided on precision approach runways with such aids as ILS. These are intended to give added texture by day and, except in fog, added texture by night in the light of

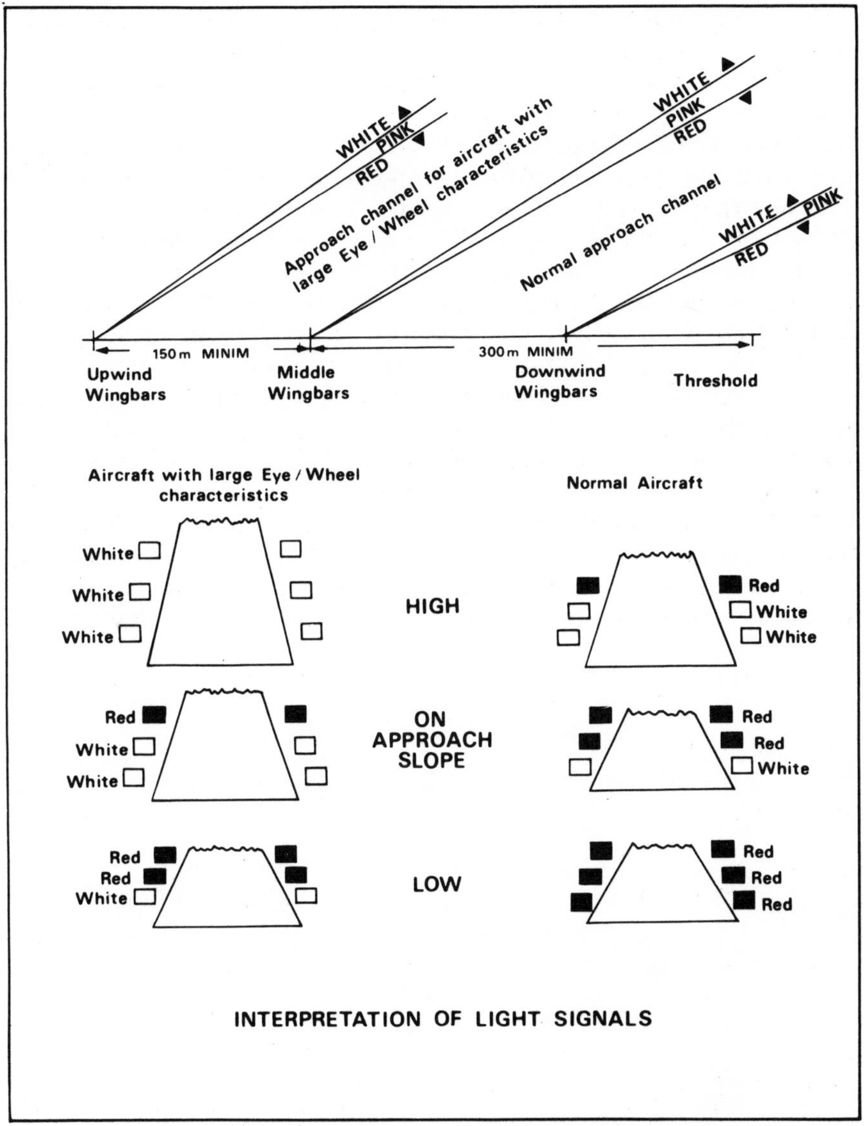

Three bar VASIs and how they are interpreted (CAA).

landing lamps. Yellow lines delineate the centres of taxyways and at certain airports self-manoeuvring stand markings enable aircraft to be taxyed to the correct parking position without the aid of a marshaller.

At airfields which accept non-radio equipped aircraft ground signals will be displayed for guidance. These are normally to be found in front of the Control Tower, but not always, which gives rise to a funny story. One day a pilot who had suffered a radio failure landed at Blackpool. On reporting to the Tower, he complained that he could not make any sense from the ground signals. Further conversation revealed that he was trying to interpret the strange shapes on the crazy Golf Course adjacent to the airport's public enclosure!

Obviously not all the following ground signals can be seen at any one airfield but they cover all those to be seen at UK civil locations. This list does not include signs peculiar to military airfields.

(*a*) Direction for landing or take-off: A large white 'T' signifies that aircraft will land or take-off in a direction parallel to the 'T' and towards the cross-arm. A white disc above the cross-arm of the 'T' indicates that the direction of landing and take-off do not necessarily coincide.

(*b*) A white 'dumb-bell' means that aircraft movement on the airfield is confined to paved surfaces only. A black strip across each disc of the dumb-bell at right angles to the shaft signifies that aircraft taking off and landing shall do so on a runway, but that ground

Standard runway markings (CAA).

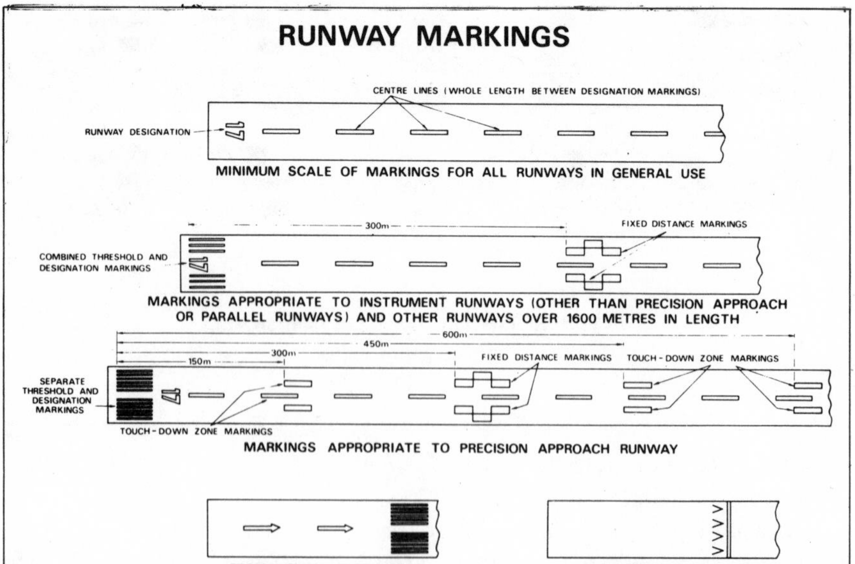

movement is not confined to paved surfaces. A red letter 'L' superimposed on the dumb-bell signifies that light aircraft are permitted to take off and land either on a runway or on the area designated by a further 'L' (painted white) elsewhere on the aerodrome.

(*c*) A red and yellow striped arrow indicates that a right hand circuit is in force. This can also be shown by a rectangular green flag flown from a mast.

(*d*) A red square with one yellow diagonal bar warns that the state of the manoeuvring area is poor and pilots must exercise special care.

(*e*) A red square with a yellow cross superimposed along the diagonals declares that the airfield is unsafe for the movement of aircraft and that landing is prohibited. (Usually found at grass airfields which are water-logged in the winter months!)

(*f*) A white letter 'H' marks the helicopter landing area.

(*g*) A double white cross signifies that glider flying is in progress. (A yellow cross indicates the tow-rope dropping area on the runway.)

(*h*) 'Aerodrome Control in operation' is shown by a red and yellow checkered flag or board. (Aircraft may only move on the manoeuvring area with ATC permission.) A black letter 'C' on a yellow board indicates the position at which a pilot can report to the ATC unit or to the person in charge of the aerodrome.

(*i*) On grass aerodromes areas of 'bad ground' are marked by triangular orange and white markers, alternating with orange and white flags. Similar coloured markers outline the aerodrome boundary.

Chapter 13

Airport operations and procedures

Vortex wake

Behind each wingtip of an aircraft in flight and, in the case of a helicopter, the tip of each rotor blade, a trailing cylinder of rapidly rotating air is created, known as a vortex. The heavier the aircraft, the more intense the effect, which is quite capable of rolling a following aircraft onto its back if it gets too close. These hazardous wake vortices begin to be generated when the nosewheel lifts off the runway on take-off and continues until it touches down on landing. To minimise the danger controllers apply a system of spacing which is outlined below.

In the United Kingdom aircraft are divided into four vortex wake categories according to their maximum total weight at take-off:

Heavy—136,000 kg or greater;
Medium—less than 136,000 kg and more than 40,000 kg;
Small—40,000 kg or less and more than 17,000 kg;
Light—17,000 kg or less.

There are, however, a few exceptions to this. Helicopters generate more intense vortices from their rotors than fixed wing aircraft of the same weight, therefore Sikorsky S61Ns and larger types are included in the small category. Several aircraft types have been grouped into vortex categories which do not conform to those listed above. For example, the Boeing 707, DC-8, VC-10 and IL-62 series have been classified as medium, as experience has shown that the characteristics of these types conform more to that group. Similarly, it has been decided to place the BAe 146 in the small category.

The medium category embraces aircraft in the BAC 111/Boeing 737/DC-9 class, together with propellor aircraft like the Hercules and

Opposite: Top *Standard Instrument Departure (SID) Chart for Runway 28 Right at Heathrow* (CAA). **Bottom** *SID Chart for Manchester Runway 24* (CAA).

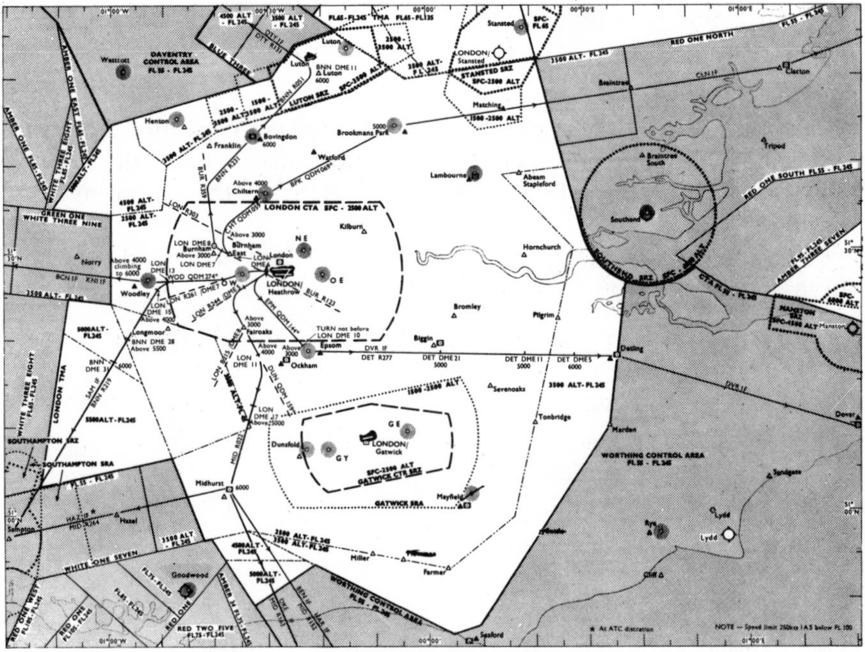

DAVENTRY CONTROL AREA FL 35 - FL 245
Westcott
Luton
Stansted
LONDON/ Stansted
STANSTED SRZ SFC-2500 ALT
RED ONE NORTH
Clacton
Braintree
Henton
Bovingdon
Brookmans Park
Franklin
Watford
Lambourne
Abeam Stapleford
Chiltern
LONDON CTA SFC - 2500 ALT
Kilburn
Burnham
LONDON/ Heathrow
Hornchurch
Southend
RED ONE SOUTH FL 55 - FL 245
Woodley
Longmoor
Bromley
Pilgrim
Fairoaks
Epsom
Ockham
Biggin
Detling
Sevenoaks
Tonbridge
Dunsfold
LONDON/ Gatwick
SFC-2500 ALT GATWICK CTR SRZ
GATWICK SRA
WORTHING CONTROL AREA FL 35 - FL 245
Mayfield
Midhurst
SOUTHAMPTON SRZ
SOUTHAMPTON SRA
WHITE ONE SEVEN
Goodwood
Hazel
Miller
Farmer
Rye
Lydd
Cliff
Dover
Manston
Seaford
RED TWO FIVE
NOTE — Speed limit 250kts IAS below FL 100
★ At ATC discretion

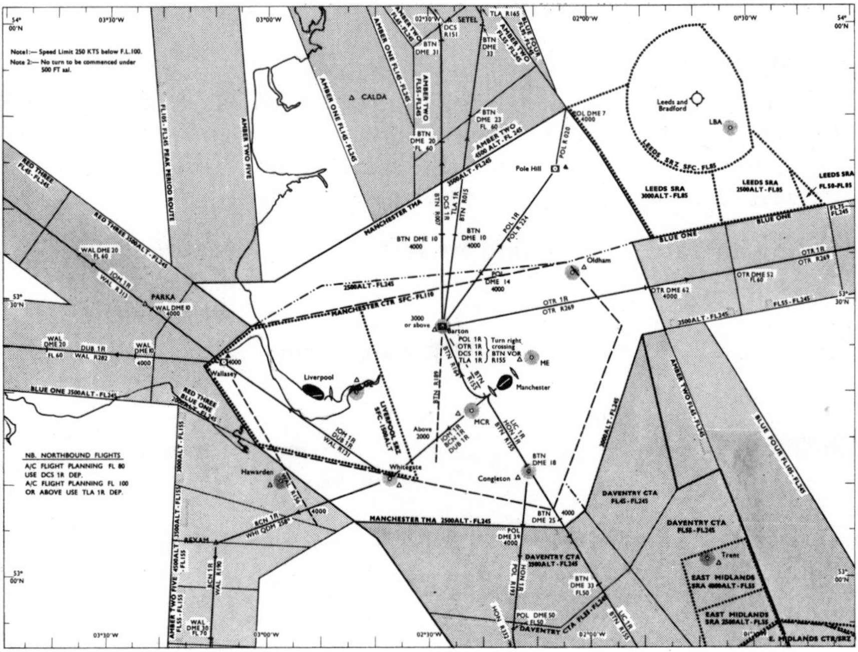

Note1:— Speed Limit 250 KTS below F.L.100.
Note 2:— No turn to be commenced under 500 FT aal.
CALDA
AMBER TWO FIVE
Leeds and Bradford
LEEDS SRZ SFC-FL85
LEEDS SRA 3000ALT - FL85
LEEDS SRA 2500ALT - FL85
Pole Hill
MANCHESTER TMA
BLUE ONE
PARKA
Oldham
MANCHESTER CTR SFC-FL110
Barton
Wallasey
Liverpool
LIVERPOOL SRZ SFC-2000ALT
Manchester
MCR
Whitegate
Hawarden
Congleton
NB. NORTHBOUND FLIGHTS
A/C FLIGHT PLANNING FL 80 USE DCS 1R DEP.
A/C FLIGHT PLANNING FL 100 OR ABOVE USE TLA 1R DEP.
MANCHESTER TMA 2500ALT-FL245
DAVENTRY CTA FL45-FL245
DAVENTRY CTA FL55-FL245
DAVENTRY CTA 3500ALT-FL245
Trent
EAST MIDLANDS SRA 4000ALT-FL55
EAST MIDLANDS SRA 2500ALT-FL55
E. MIDLANDS CTR/SRZ

Vanguard. Small includes the Viscount, Friendship, and Herald and light anything from executive jets downwards.

Arriving Flights

Where flights are operating visually (IFR flights operating under the reduced minima in the vicinity of aerodromes, VFR flights, or a mixture of the two), pilots are to be informed of the recommended spacing.

For other flights the spacing listed below is to be applied between successive aircraft on final approach.

Leading aircraft	Following aircraft	Minimum distance
Heavy	Heavy	4 miles
	Medium	5 miles
	Small	6 miles
	Light	8 miles
Medium	Medium	3 miles
	Small	4 miles
	Light	6 miles
Small	Medium or small	3 miles
	Light	4 miles

Aerodrome Operations

The minimum spacing listed below is to be applied between successive aircraft, both IFR and VFR flights.

(*a*) Aircraft departing from the same runway or from parallel runways less than 760 m apart (including grass strips).

Leading aircraft	Following aircraft		Minimum spacing at time aircraft are airborne
Heavy	Medium Small Light	Departing from the same take-off position	2 minutes
Medium or small	Light	Departing from the same take-off position	2 minutes
Heavy (Full length take-off)	Medium Small Light	Departing from an intermediate take-off point	3 minutes

Medium or small	Light	Departing from an intermediate take-off point	3 minutes

(*b*) Operations on a runway with a displaced landing threshold if the projected flight paths are expected to cross.

Leading aircraft	**Following aircraft**		**Minimum spacing at time aircraft are airborne or have touched down**
Heavy arrival	Medium Small Light	departure	2 minutes
Heavy departure	Medium Small Light	arrival	2 minutes

(*c*) Operations on crossing and diverging runways or on parallel runways greater than 760 m apart.

The spacings below are to be applied whenever the projected flight paths of the aircraft cross.

Leading aircraft	**Aircraft crossing behind**	**Minimum distance**	**Time equivalent**
Heavy	Heavy	4 miles	2 minutes
	Medium	5 miles	3 minutes
	Small	6 miles	3 minutes
	Light	8 miles	4 minutes
Medium	Medium	3 miles	2 minutes
	Small	4 miles	2 minutes
	Light	6 miles	3 minutes
Small	Medium or small	3 miles	2 minutes
	Light	4 miles	2 minutes

(*d*) Opposite direction runway operations. A minimum of two minutes spacing is to be provided from the time a heavy aircraft making a low or missed approach crosses over the take-off position of a medium, small or light aircraft departing from the opposite direction runway.

En-route and Intermediate Approach

No special longitudinal spacings based on time are required. When a medium, small or light aircraft is positioned by radar to cross behind or follow the same track as a heavy aircraft, the minimum spacing shall be 5 miles.

Departure flow regulation

At airports handling international traffic one will hear frequent references on the Tower or Ground Movement frequencies to Approved Departure Times. These were known previously as 'slot times' and this term is sometimes heard as well. During the peak summer months some countries are unable, for a number of reasons, to cope with the extra traffic. For instance, over 50 European and 27 UK airports are currently sending aircraft to the Mediterranean. Spain has about nine airports to receive the majority of them, with Palma the most popular destination. When the number of aircraft wishing to fly outstrips the capacity of the foreign ATC systems, the flow of traffic has to be regulated to ensure safe separation both nationally and internationally. This means that aircraft have to be held on the ground at the departure airports until such time as they can be accepted.

In the early 1970s a Departure Flow Regulation (DFR) section was set up at LATCC, operating 24 hours a day and manned by two controllers and one assistant. They now provide departure times about two hours ahead for up to 800 aircraft per day. This ensures an organised system of queuing for all flights as well as enabling airlines to plan aircraft and crew utilisation. When the ATC system in any part of Europe is in danger of being overloaded, a queue starts to form as a result of delaying departure times and so a list of airways with DFR restrictions is published in a NOTAM well in advance of the summer season.

For the uninitiated, the term Notam is an abbreviation of Notice to Airmen and is defined as 'a notice containing information concerning the establishment, condition or change of any facility, service, procedure or hazard, the timely knowledge of which is essential for the safe and efficient operation of aircraft.' There are two classes of Notam; Class One being distributed by telex, Class Two, less urgent, being sent out by post.

Complications arise as different airways have different restrictions depending on destination, Flight Level or routeing, and countries overflown. If the system becomes overloaded, the flow of traffic has to be reduced. The DFR controller thus has the responsibility of allocating the correct number of aircraft at the intervals prescribed for a particular airway, route, Flight Level or destination.

The ADT stipulates that an aircraft must not be airborne before a specified time, but an allowance of six minutes is added to this to cover taxying delays or holding for landing traffic. This can cause the GMC or Tower Controller something of a headache as extra-careful planning is often necessary to make sure that the aircraft gets away on time. The situation is not helped by pilots who taxy excruciatingly slowly or arrive at the runway threshold five minutes before the ADT!

Noise abatement

In an effort to minimise noise nuisance to local residents most airports have their own noise abatement procedures. These are devised by the aerodrome operating authority in conjunction with airlines and local airport consultative committees. Over built-up areas minimum noise routes have been defined which carefully route aircraft away from the more densely populated areas. Engine climb power is also reduced for the period when the aircraft must fly over certain conurbations.

At Heathrow different parallel runways are used for take-off and landing and these are alternated regularly so that noise is spread more equitably over the areas beneath the flight paths. Runways 28 Left and 28 Right are the preferred ones, provided the tail wind component does not exceed a certain figure and, in addition, flights are severely restricted at night. At Manchester the direction of approach is changed at regular intervals and at both locations noise levels are monitored. Operators whose aircraft exceed the permitted values are penalised.

Minimum Noise Routes (MNRs) are integrated with the lower end of Standard Instrument Departures, which are themselves designed to cause the least disturbance to those living below. Similarly, Continuous Descent Approaches are being brought into operation, particularly at Heathrow, to reduce noise and, as a bonus, to speed up the arrival rate. Headings and Flight Levels at which aircraft are to leave the holding pattern are passed by ATC. On receipt of descent clearance the pilot descends at the rate he judges to be best suited to achieve continuous descent. The object is to join the glide path at the appropriate height for the distance without recourse to level flight.

The procedure requires that aircraft fly at 210 kt during the intermediate approach phase. ATC may request speed reductions to within the band 160 kt to 180 kt on, or shortly before, the closing heading to the ILS and 160 kt when established on the ILS. Aircraft unable to conform to these speeds are expected to inform ATC and state which speeds they are able to use. Since wheels and flaps remain retracted until the final stages, less engine power is needed which results in a much quieter approach.

Standard Instrument Departures (SIDs)

SIDs have been developed for the main runways of major airports, the routes terminating at an airway, Advisory Route or at a radio navigational fix. Minimum Noise Routes are also built in. All aircraft departing from an airport under IFR are required to follow the appropriate SID, unless and until authorised to do otherwise by the relevant ATC unit.

Each SID for a particular runway has a designator which incorporates the name of the radio beacon on which it is based. An example is the Honiley One Tango from Runway 27 at Liverpool:

Straight ahead to Wallasey DME 9, turn left to intercept Wallasey VOR Radial 134. At Wallasey DME 24 turn right onto Honiley Radial 332 to Honiley VOR.

VOR/DME Holding Chart Willo for Gatwick (CAA).

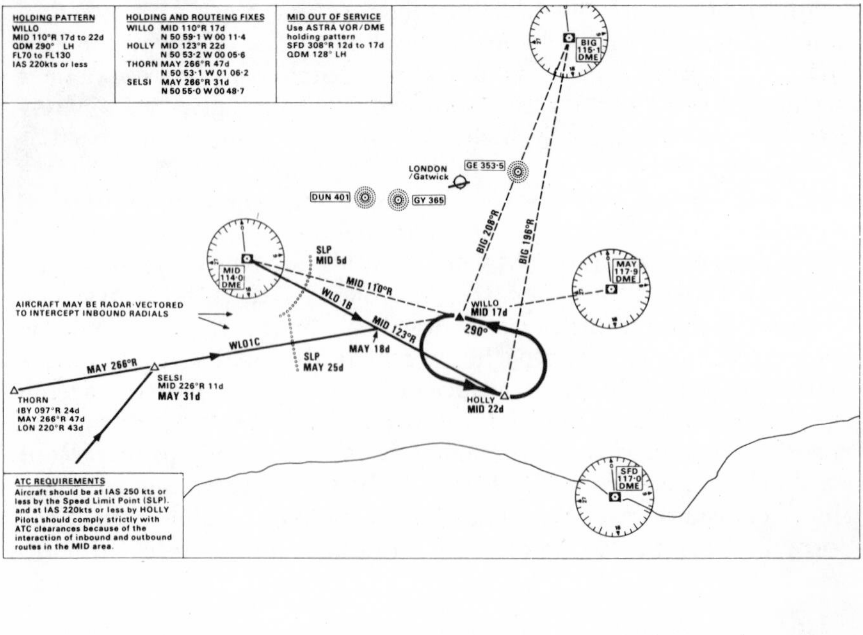

The heights to be observed are:

Cross Wallasey DME 17 3,000 ft or above. Cross Wallasey DME 28 at 4,000 ft. Cross Honiley DME 45 at FL 50.

VOR/DME holding procedures

These procedures are already in extensive use in the USA and are now being introduced into the United Kingdom. An example is DAYNE, south of Manchester Airport, an 'offset' holding pattern for traffic inbound to Manchester and Woodford. Its axis is aligned on Trent VOR Radial 315, its position between Trent DME 13 and 17 miles.

The pilot flies towards the VOR/DME on this designated inbound radial and on reaching the holding fix position carries out a procedure turn onto the reciprocal outbound track. This outbound track is flown until the limiting DME distance is attained and the pilot then turns the aircraft to intercept the inbound VOR radial back to the holding fix position.

In the event of a ground equipment failure at the VOR/DME installation, a standby procedure is published, based on an alternative VOR/DME or other radio beacon. In the case of DAYNE, the holding pattern is defined additionally by a radial and distance from the Manchester VOR/DME.

Aircraft type and airfield designators

For flight planning and flight progress strip presentation aircraft types have been allocated a designator of not more than four characters, by ICAO. Where possible this conforms to the manufacturer's designation, or at least to part of it. For example Boeing 707, 737, 747 are represented by B707, B737 and B747, an HS74 is an HS 748, an SH36 a Shorts 360, and an S210 a Caravelle.

The codes are often used on R/T, most being fairly obvious, but some are obscure. Controllers occasionally ask a pilot for his aircraft type and get an answer which is not very enlightening. Space does not permit a comprehensive listing which would run into many hundreds of entries, but commonly heard designators are listed in Appendix 4.

One other point is the use of four-letter designators for airfields. These are rarely heard on R/T but are allocated by ICAO on a worldwide basis for flight planning and telex purposes. British airfields are prefixed 'EG', hence EGLL—Heathrow, EGKK—Gatwick and EGCC—Manchester. A few European examples are EDDH—Hamburg, LFPO—Paris Orly, EBOS—Ostend, LSZH—Zurich and LEMD—Madrid. American airports are prefixed 'K', as in KJFK—Kennedy, KLAX—Los Angeles.

Chapter 14

Royal Flights

Royal Flight status is sometimes extended to other reigning sovereigns, Prime Ministers and other Heads of State as a courtesy. Contrary to popular opinion, there are no special increased separations for Royal flights; they are treated exactly the same as any other aircraft in controlled airspace, although a certain amount of priority is given where necessary as the Royal personage usually has to meet a tight schedule.

Royal flights in fixed wing aircraft are always provided with controlled airspace to cover the entire flight path when it is within UK airspace. This coverage is obtained by the establishment of Purple airways for the entire route and special Control Zones at the departure and destination airfields if these are not already in existence. Purple airways normally extend five miles either side of the route and may coincide with existing airways of the national system. The vertical dimensions, relevant radio frequencies, times and any other pertinent information will be detailed in the NOTAM concerning the flight.

The NOTAM is prepared by the Airspace Utilisation Section whenever a Royal flight is arranged. It is distributed by post to the ATCCs and airfields concerned, normally providing at least 48 hours' warning. All Purple airspace is notified as Rule 21, ie any aircraft within it must fly by IFR at all times. In the case of temporary Control Zones, ATC may issue Special VFR clearances to pilots unable to comply with the IFR requirements and thus ensure positive separation at all times.

Purple airspace is not normally established for Royal helicopter flights but a Royal Low Level Corridor, marked by a series of check-points, is promulgated. These check-points will be approximately 20 miles apart and will usually coincide with turning points on the route. Pilots flying near the Corridor are expected to keep a good look-out and maintain adequate separation from the Royal helicopter. The NOTAM will incorporate a list of nominated aerodromes from which pilots may obtain information on the progress of the flight.

Royal flights are readily identifiable by their distinctive callsigns. 'Kittyhawk' is used when HM the Queen is on board, 'Rainbow' the Duke of Edinburgh, 'Unicorn' the Prince of Wales and 'Leopard' for Prince Andrew. The prefix 'Kitty' and a number is employed when other members of the Royal family are being carried and also for positioning and training flights.

Chapter 15

Air displays

From an ATC point of view, displays are fairly straightforward to control provided that the organisers have scheduled the items in a sensible order. Proper pre-planning in liaison with ATC is essential to avoid non-radio light aircraft clashing with jet aerobatic teams and similar embarrassments. I have known pilots without radio over-running their time slot and either ignoring or failing to see frantic lamp signals from the Tower while a Buccaneer or some such fast jet orbits in the distance with fuel dwindling rapidly. On another occasion we were horrified to see a formation of Turbulents take-off without permission while the Red Arrows were still performing. Fortunately they were on their final manoeuvre and to the crowd it probably looked like brilliant timing!

Timing is of course paramount to the continuity of a display. How many times do we hear the complaint that there were long gaps, causing the crowd to lose interest? The usual reason is that almost inevitably one or more of the items on the programme fails to turn up. Vintage aircraft are particularly temperamental, although their modern brethren can be just as bad. It thus becomes a major operation to close up the vacant slots and there are a number of ways this can be done. Since many shows now average 3–4 hours in duration and always seem to run late after the first hour or so, some of the time can be absorbed with ease. Pilots can usually be coaxed into extending their individual demonstrations slightly and it is not unknown for airline passengers to find themselves taking part if they happen to be arriving aboard a schedule during the show! ATC is normally in radio contact with a display co-ordinator who can communicate directly with the pilots on the flight line who are waiting their turn to perform. Rapid reshuffling is therefore possible but it often leads to some heated exchanges on the air!

Ideally, the next aircraft on the programme should be taking off as the previous one turns final, leaving no break in the proceedings. (The Farnborough shows have always been noted for this smooth flow.) Aircraft approaching from other airfields are held either on radar or at a distinctive and usually pre-arranged geographical position until they can be fitted in. I have witnessed high performance aircraft like the F-15 hold in the overhead at 10,000 ft or so and arrive almost vertically.

R/T is kept to a minimum during airshows; the last thing a pilot wants is unnecessary chatter during a complex sequence. He is usually advised the number of minutes to go as his slot nears its end and is expected to abide by this. The aircraft type is quite often used as a callsign but military aircraft, apart from the Battle of Britain Memorial Flight as one example, normally employ their RAF or USAF callsigns. Since many military aircraft, particularly fighters, are only UHF-equipped, you will obviously not hear them talking to ATC on VHF. Portable UHF equipment will have been installed in the Tower at civil airfields for the occasion.

Aerobatic teams generally have their own discrete frequency although the leader will be monitoring the Tower channel in case there are any panic calls about a lost Cessna 150 blundering through the area! (It happens...) Orders from the Red Arrows' leader are a miracle of brevity on the R/T—'Smoke on go' being an oft-quoted example.

Far more entertaining is airband listening during the morning before an air display when some of the participants arrive and mingle with visiting aircraft, pleasure flights and the inevitable club pilot who wants to get in a few circuits before being grounded for the rest of the day. The results approach chaos and one feels for the Tower Controllers who are trying to sort it all out. I once had to scatter everybody to different points of the compass to allow four Jet Provosts low on fuel to make a priority landing. Another time a Bonanza's nose wheel collapsed and a non-radio Tiger Moth was dissuaded from landing on top of him by a quick-draw red flare!

Nowadays, air races are often sandwiched into air displays and are quite popular with ATC because we can sit back and watch, leaving the starting to the race marshallers. The drama comes at the end of the race when, if the handicappers have done a good job, 15 to 20 aircraft are all downwind for landing at the same time. Since it is impossible to apply normal rules for runway occupancy to this congestion, controllers tend to opt out of the situation by giving wind checks and muttering 'Land at your discretion' and similar platitudes to pilots who call on final. Half the aircraft may be non-radio anyway and, as race pilots' airmanship is usually pretty good, they can safely be left to themselves to sort things out.

With the numbers of air displays in Britain increasing every year, the CAA have issued a booklet for the guidance of organisers. This is CAP 403 *Safety Arrangements at Flying Displays, Air Races and Rallies.* The reader is also recommended to sample David Ogilvy's book *Flying Displays* (Airlife Publications) for an excellent guide to the pitfalls of their organisation and running.

Chapter 16

Emergencies

Emergency situations with aircraft are fairly common and although the word conjures up images of catastrophic failure or fire in the air, few are very dramatic, even if they do give the pilot some worrying moments. The most numerous are cockpit indications of undercarriage malfunctions which may necessitate a low run past the Tower for a visual check that the wheels are down. There is no guarantee that they are locked, though, but it gives the pilot some encouragement! Almost invariably the green lights come on when the jolt of the landing activates a stuck micro-switch.

Other frequent problems are doors coming open in flight, failed generators and lost fuel filler caps. On most light aircraft an open door is a noisy and draughty inconvenience rather than an actual hazard but there are some types on which the adverse effect on the airflow can reduce control. Hence, unlike in the USA where a pilot has formally to declare an emergency before the safety services are alerted, a British controller uses his own judgment and almost always puts them on a Local Standby, working on the saying 'Better safe than sorry'. There is also the possibility that a minor problem with the aircraft may distract a pilot enough to make him misjudge the landing.

There are six standard categories of emergency beginning with the self-explanatory 'Aircraft Accident'. A 'Full Emergency' is arranged when it is known that an aircraft is, or is suspected to be, in such trouble that there is a danger of an accident. The problems include the thankfully rare fire in the air and the not uncommon engine failure on multi-engined aircraft. In the latter case an experienced and properly trained commercial pilot should have no difficulty in making a safe landing as he is required to practice asymmetric flying at regular intervals and pass a check. The safety services are alerted, however, and at larger airports this usually means the outside services will be summoned automatically as a back-up.

Next comes the 'Local Standby' which I have mentioned already and the 'Aircraft Ground Incident' which covers occurrences other than accidents. These include fuel spillages and bomb scares on parked aircraft. A 'Weather Standby' is instituted 'when weather conditions are such as to render a landing difficult or difficult to observe.' Bad visibility is one obvious instance, a cross-wind component of 25 kt or more is another. The final category is 'Domestic Fire' which, as its title implies, covers such things as grass fires on and adjacent to the airfield and fires in its buildings.

A pilot requiring immediate assistance is expected to transmit a distress message with the prefix 'Mayday, Mayday, Mayday'. If the situation is less urgent the prefix 'Pan, Pan, Pan' is used. Unfortunately, pilots, particularly phlegmatic British ones, are loath to make too much of a fuss so if you hear a 'Mayday' call, things have really reached the critical stage! The announcement of the loss of one engine, provided there are more than one, is usually delivered in a matter-of-fact manner, together with a request for a diversion. This calm approach is sometimes self-defeating—a controller who would be sparked into instant action to clear a path for an aircraft which has abruptly turned into a glider in the circuit, may think he has misheard if the magic word 'Mayday' is not used and waste time asking for a repeat. I once admonished a pilot for approaching the wrong runway only to be told that he was distracted by an oil warning light and wanted to land as soon as possible. Of course, he had never mentioned this over the radio! If he had, he would have got all the priority he needed.

Aircraft in distress or lost, if they are not already in two-way contact with an ATC unit, may call on the International Distress Frequency of 121.5 Mhz. If they have a transponder the code 7700 can be selected to indicate an emergency. (This activates an alarm at every radar station able to receive the signal and also makes the radar blip pulsate to attract the controller's attention.) The Distress Frequency is monitored continuously by the RAF Distress and Diversion Cell at West Drayton in Middlesex and at Prestwick in Scotland, which serve the areas south and north of 55°N, respectively. They can provide a service to civil aircraft in emergency in addition to that for military aircraft on 243 Mhz UHF.

South of a line from Preston to the Humber there is a reasonable chance of fixing the position of aircraft at quite low levels transmitting on 121.5, except over the hilly areas of Wales and South-West England. This 'Fixer Service', as it is known, takes bearings automatically from several receivers and projects them as lines on a large wall map. Where they intersect is the aircraft's position and remarkable accuracy can be achieved. Most of the larger airports keep the distress frequency selected and are thus able to hear any calls and relay bearing information to the D & D Cell if requested.

Pilots are encouraged to make practice Pan calls on 121.5, having first of all asked permission in case there is a real emergency in progress. It is extremely impressive to hear how quickly D & D can fix the aircraft's position. Aircraft on transatlantic flights are required to monitor 121.5 continuously and there have been many occasions when a high-flying airliner has relayed distress messages from some wave-hopping light aircraft on a delivery flight and alerted the rescue services.

Transmissions from aircraft in distress have priority over all other messages. When a pilot is already in contact with an ATC unit, assistance should be sought on the frequency in use, otherwise a call should be made on 121.5. On hearing a distress call, all stations must maintain radio silence on that frequency unless they themselves are required to render assistance and should continue to listen on the frequency concerned until it is evident that assistance is being provided.

The recommended form of the distress message to be transmitted is somewhat long-winded and it would have to be a very cool pilot who remembered to include everything (and in the right order!) even assuming he had time to make the full call. I have heard three; they were all in the circuit area and all there was time to say was Mayday three times, callsign and 'Engine failure'. Two of them got down safely but the helicopter crashed, although not too badly I'm glad to say.

The information to be passed goes like this:

(*a*) Name of the station addressed (when appropriate)
(*b*) Callsign and type of aircraft
(*c*) Nature of the emergency
(*d*) Intention of the person in command
(*e*) Present position, Flight Level/altitude and heading
(f) Pilot's qualifications as appropriate: (1) Student pilot; (2) No instrument qualification; (3) IMC rated; (4) Full Instrument Rating.

Pilots are invited to use the callsign prefix 'TYRO' when calling a military ATC unit or the D & D Section, to indicate lack of experience. This code word will ensure that controllers do not issue instructions which the pilot may have difficulty in following.

The standard acknowledgment is 'GABCD (station) Roger Mayday.' Further instructions follow without delay. It may be necessary to impose radio silence on all stations in the area or any particular station which, usually unintentionally having just come onto the frequency, interferes with emergency transmissions. In either case the messages should take this form: 'All stations Hurn Approach stop transmitting, Mayday' or 'GAMPT stop transmitting, Mayday'.

It may be a good idea to transfer aircraft from the frequency to avoid interfering with calls from or to the aircraft in distress. 'Mayday. All stations contact Hurn Tower on 125.6. Out.' When an emergency situation has been resolved, the station which has been controlling the traffic will broadcast a message that normal working will be resumed. 'Mayday all stations Hurn Approach time 04 distress traffic GABCD ended. Out.'

When an aircraft is operating on a flight plan and fails to turn up within 30 minutes of its ETA, the controller at the destination is required to confirm the ATD (actual time of departure) from the departure airfield. Other set procedures known as Preliminary Overdue Action are put into effect. After one hour, or sooner in certain cases, Full Overdue Action is taken by the parent ATCC and a search launched for the missing aircraft.

Aircraft on a flight for which a plan has not been filed have no such protection, although they are required to 'Book out' with the ATC unit at the departure aerodrome, assuming one exists. The departure, together with time en route, fuel endurance and number of souls on board, are recorded but no further action need be taken and if an aircraft goes missing, it is often some time before people start asking questions, usually sparked off by anxious relatives.

Flight plans must be filed at least 30 minutes before requesting taxy clearance or start-up approval. A pilot may file one for any flight but for certain categories they are mandatory. These include all IFR flights within controlled airspace, those which cross an international boundary, and for any flight where the destination is more than 40 km from the aerodrome of departure and the aircraft's maximum total weight exceeds 5,700 kg. In addition, a pilot is advised to file a plan if he intends to fly over the sea more than ten miles from the coast or over sparsely populated areas where search and rescue operations would be difficult.

For scheduled airline routes and other regularly recurring IFR flights with identical basic features, a repetitive flight plan saves operators and crews the chore of filing a separate plan each time. Often referred to as a 'stored plan', it is submitted by an operator for storage and repetitive use by ATC units for each individual flight.

Airmisses

Now, a word about airmisses, which the press prefers to call 'nearmisses'. A pilot is entitled to file an Airmiss Report when he considers that his aircraft may have been endangered by the proximity of another aircraft in flight, to the extent that a definite risk of collision existed. A sense of proportion is required for this, however, as light aircraft in traffic circuits occasionally get horrendously close to one another, usually through inexperience and/or not keeping a good look-out.

Pilots flying under IFR in controlled airspace may well file if they see another aircraft which they believe is closer to them than required by the separation rules. In a radar-controlled environment this may be four instead of five miles, which a pilot flying under VFR would consider ludicrous.

All Airmiss Reports are investigated, not so much as to allot blame but to try to prevent a recurrence by examining the circumstances. The degree of actual risk of collision is assessed and regular summaries of the most serious ones are published for restricted circulation in the aviation world. Inevitably, some are leaked to the press and suitably exaggerated! One they never heard about unfortunately was the large pink pig which an Army helicopter pilot nearly rammed one hazy day over the River Thames. It was an advertising balloon which had broken its moorings and drifted away!

Radio failures

If an aircraft suffers a radio failure there are published procedures to which the pilot is expected to adhere. A squawk of 7600 set on the transponder will alert an ATC unit to his problem, provided that it has SSR capability. If essential navigation equipment has failed also, pilots are advised as a last resort to carry out a special procedure to alert the Radar Controller to the fact that they need assistance. The aircraft is to fly at least two triangular patterns, before resuming course, as follows:

Aircraft speed	Length of leg	Transmitter failure only	Complete failure
300 kt or less	2 minutes	Right hand turns	Left hand turns
More than 300 kt	1 minute		

If the controller should notice such a manoeuvre (and RAF experiments show that they often do not!) he is to advise the Distress & Diversion Cell of the position and track and continue to plot the aircraft whilst it is in radar cover. A shepherd aircraft will then be sent out to lead it, hopefully, to a safe landing.

Quite often the failure is of the transmitter only and the controller can instruct the aircraft to make one or more turns and check if the pilot is complying. If it becomes obvious that the receiver is working, normal radar service is resumed. There are some subtle ways by which the aircraft's altitude and other information can be ascertained, such as 'After passing FL 50 turn left heading 270.'

There are occasions when an aircraft receiver is working correctly but the reply transmitted is unintelligible at the ground station because the speech is badly distorted or non-existent, perhaps because the microphone is unserviceable. Military pilots are briefed to use a special code which makes use of the carrier wave only. The pilot presses his transmitter button a certain number of times according to the following code:

One short transmission—Yes (or an acknowledgement);

Two short transmissions—No;

Three short transmissions—Say again:

Four short transmissions—Request homing;

One long transmission (two seconds)—Manoeuvre complete (eg, steady on heading);

One long, two short, one long—The aircraft has developed another emergency.

A controller will be alerted to the presence of an aircraft with this kind of failure if he hears, or sees on the VDF, four short carrier wave transmissions. The controller should then interrogate the pilot, using the callsign 'Speechless Aircraft' if the identity of the aircraft cannot be discovered, to find out what assistance is required. He must be careful to ask questions which can be answered with a direct yes or no. The code is now recommended for use by civilian pilots as it can easily be explained by the controller during the first few transmissions.

Chapter 17

Air band radios

In the early days of air band radios back in the 1960s, there were only two or three types available. The variety then grew steadily, prices came down and some were miniaturised to true pocket size. Manufacturers came and went, some to obscurity, others to the more lucrative field of two-way communications equipment. Today, the potential purchaser is faced with a bewildering selection of sets from around £10 up to well over £400.

I do not intend to give a *Which?* Magazine type of survey on the best to buy as I have not had the opportunity to test all those listed. Nor have I included all the cheap models stocked by various high street outlets; some of these are excellent, but beware of those which purport to cover the air band but stop at 130 Mhz, thus depriving you of the upper section of the band.

The irritating drawback with nearly all the cheaper receivers is the lack of an accurate tuning facility, so you are never quite sure to which frequency you are tuned until you have listened for a while. The problem is solved (at a price!) by buying a set with an LCD or LED display showing the frequency currently being monitored. Unfortunately, there is still a tendency for the signal to 'drift' if the radio is left on the same frequency for a time and it then has to be retuned.

This too can be eradicated by the use of crystal-controlled receiver channels, using pre-selected crystals for the frequencies you wish to monitor regularly. You can either select one of these or, with volume set and squelch, where fitted, turned down to eliminate carrier wave 'hiss', the radio can be left on to scan the frequencies, automatically over-riding the squelch whenever there is a transmission. Squelch, by the way, is a method of suppressing unwanted background noise from the receiver by reducing its sensitivity.

There are a great number of features on today's sets and it is obviously important to find out exactly what is or is not included in the purchase price. Some require separate aerials, others power supplies and battery chargers.

Some of the sets can be used in a vehicle but only receive signals which are above the locally-generated 'noise'. A good check is to set the squelch control to the just quiet position. With the vehicle aerial extended, plug in and then start the engine. The ignition and dynamo/alternator 'noise' will override the squelch setting and this will have to be advanced to quiet the monitor in the new local 'noise' condition. Adequate suppression of the ignition is necessary to ensure a reasonable performance. When travelling close to buildings the receiver will 'chop', this is due to multi-path reflections from the various surrounding objects.

Another important consideration is the length of the receiver scale. On a short one of about 2 in if, say, 124.2 is tuned in, transmissions on the adjacent frequencies of 124.0, 124.05, 124.10, 124.15 and 124.25, 124.30, 124.35 and so on, may be picked up as well. They are not usually as loud as the primary frequency being monitored but are irritating and confusing, particularly when a powerful transmission from a nearer source swamps the aircraft in which you are interested. This overlapping effect is minimised where a longer scale is provided.

All the specialised dealers hold stocks of accessories, such as headphones, earpieces, spare crystals, battery chargers and assorted plugs, leads and adaptors. A number of different types of aerial are offered, including some for loft or outside mounting. Many of the dealers also sell official airways charts and guides.

As has been stated before, VHF reception is 'quasi-line of sight' so the higher the aerial the better the result. As most air band listening will probably be done at home, it is useful to discover the best position for reception by moving the set around the house. Radio waves behave in a very peculiar fashion and marked differences will be found even in the same room. If the usual telescopic aerial fitted to the cheaper sets proves inadequate, a remote antenna can be purchased, or alternatively an aerial can be made at home quite cheaply. Any amateur radio book from the local library will tell you how to do this.

The newcomer to air band listening is recommended to purchase one of the more inexpensive sets first to familiarise him or herself with what is being said and its meaning. When hooked on air band (and it does not take very long!) one can move on to a more ambitious receiver. Second hand models are often advertised in the aviation magazines, particularly the 'Freeads' column in *Aviation News*.

Air band radios currently available

NB Prices may vary as currencies fluctuate.

Price range: £10—£20

Flight 35 Air/AM/FM/CB bands; *Flight 85* Air/AM/FM/CB bands; *Harvard* Air/AM/FM bands; *Ingersoll* Air/AM/FM/CB bands; *Jetstream* Air/FM bands; Phillips D 1007 Air/AM/FM bands; *Skyway* Air/AM/FM bands; Shira GR8388 Air/FM/AM bands; Texet HH925 Air/FM/MW/LW bands; Steepletone Air/FM/MW/LW bands.

Price Range: £50—£60

Signal R537—A good compromise if financial constraints preclude buying one of the much more expensive crystal-controlled sets. It combines a tuneable dial covering 118 Mhz to 136 Mhz with two selectable channels which are crystal-controlled. Having decided which two frequencies you monitor most often, perhaps the Tower at a local airport plus an airways frequency, you can order these with your set. As well as its internal batteries, it has the facility to operate from an external nine volt supply. Other advantages are its very small size and low weight, which make it a true pocket model.

Price range: Around £110

Signal R528—This has six crystal-controlled channels. Channels 1, 2 and 3 are scanned continuously and a fourth channel is switch-selected from any one of the remaining three. If there is a signal on any of the four frequencies being scanned, the set will lock on to it automatically. The reason for only scanning four channels out of the six is that ATIS, VOLMET, etc on which there is virtually continuous transmission, cause the set to lock on to these frequencies if they are incorporated into the set. Therefore they can be put in channels 4, 5 or 6 and only switched in when required. The makers point out, with some truth, that in the vast majority of cases six channels are perfectly adequate. For example, 1—your local airport approach, 2—the Tower, 3—radar, 4—local airways, 5—another airways frequency, 6—well, you see what they mean! The crystals are, however, simple to change, no tuning is required, so you can always have extra channels.

Price range: £120—£150

Fairmate AS 32320—As well as VHF broadcast bands, this set covers the air band and also the military UHF band from 296 Mhz to 367 Mhz. Two sets of ten memories means that desired frequencies can be pre-programmed and scanned on demand. Similarly, the entire band can be scanned if preferred. Note that a telescopic aerial is not supplied.

Price range: £175—£200

Signal R532—Covers 1040 channels in 25 Khz steps (110 Mhz to 136 Mhz). Up to 100 frequencies can be programmed into the memory and scanned at will. LED display. Can hold in its memory up to 100 different frequencies which are stored in ten banks of ten. They can easily be scanned or used to monitor a specific frequency. Rechargeable batteries and flexible aerial.

The problem of poor scale accuracy on tuneable air band radios has been solved by making the set fully tuneable on Channel 1 by a large edge-type knob, from 108 Mhz to 136 Mhz, but its oscillator is coupled to a large five digit (two decimal place) LCD read-out, so if you want to monitor Manchester Approach, for example, on 119.40, just turn the knob until the frequency reads this. If you want to tune the Tower on 118.70 adjust the knob until the read-out shows the required frequency.

Price range: £200–£250

Uniden Bearcat 100XL—Air/FM/PSB hand-held scanner with 16 channels programmable. Other features include a method of setting upper and lower limits of search range and an automatic lock-out which skips channels not of current interest for a faster scanning cycle.

Uniden Bearcat 175XL—Air/FM/PSB desk-mounted scanner with 16 channel programme and a great many features, which include an adjustable scan speed, four hours of memory protection in case of power failure and a priority mode which samples the frequency on channel one every three seconds.

Price range: £250—£300

REVCO RS2000—A 70 channel automatic VHF/UHF/FM scanner with two-speed scan and search. The advanced search feature allows unknown signals to be captured and monitored and their frequencies to be stored automatically in the memory for later recall.

Sony Air 7—A very compact portable whose small size belies its great potential. Air, AM, FM and PSB coverage, 10 memory presets for each band. Scanning can be either all ten or any lesser combination with 'priority' possible on any selected channel. This enables the user to concentrate on a particular frequency whilst still monitoring the rest.

Super Pro—Covers VHF, UHF and FM bands both scanning and manual. 20 channels. Memory retention when switched off. 12 volt car operation or via mains adaptor for home use.

Price range: Around £490

AR 2002—This Rolls-Royce of VHF/UHF monitors gives continued coverage from 25 Mhz to 550 Mhz. It has a digital display of frequency, mode and a memory channel. No crystals are required, the desired frequencies being programmed in. A search facility is included between two designated frequencies which the user can alter at will. Two speeds of search are available, and the receiver has the ability to scan frequencies from low to high and vice versa. So that nothing is missed, a delay function can be switched in to cope with the slight pause between transmissions when listening to a two-way conversation. A pre-set priority frequency is held by Channel 1 and monitored at two-second intervals. As if this were not enough, there is also a built-in digital clock!

Principal air band suppliers

Fairbotham & Co Ltd, 58-62 Lower Hillgate, Stockport, Cheshire SK1 3AN. Telephone 061-480-4872

Langtons Radio, High Street, Rocester, Staffordshire ST14 5JU. Telephone 0889 590388

Lowe Electronics Ltd, Chesterfield Road, Matlock, Derbyshire DE4 5LE. Telephone 0629 2817 *and* 162 High Street, Chesterton, Cambridge CB9 1NL. Telephone 0223 311230

Stewart Aviation, PO Box 7, Market Harborough, Leicesterhsire LE16 8XL. Telephone 0536 770962

South West Air Band Radios, Camberley House, South Knighton, Newton Abbot, Devon TQ12 6NP. Telephone Bickington 661

Waters and Stanton, 18 Main Road, Hockley, Essex. Telephone 0702 206835

Chapter 18

Charts and related documents

Almost as important as an air band radio itself is the acquisition of a set of radio navigation charts. These are essential to build up an overall picture of the UK airways system and the positions of its beacons and reporting points.

En route charts are published by three organisations for the United Kingdom; the Royal Air Force, British Airways Aerad and Jeppesen. The USAF produces its own charts but these are more difficult to obtain. Obviously the information on the different charts is fundamentally the same, but the presentation differs quite considerably. There is also some variation in the areas covered and only the RAF charts for the United Kingdom show the whole of the British Isles on one sheet. This is separated into two charts, 411H for high altitudes and 412S/412N for low altitudes. The low level charts are drawn to an approximate scale of 14 nautical miles to the inch, while the high level ones are about 28 nautical miles to the inch.

British Airways Aerad charts for the United Kingdom cover high altitude (H109/108) at a scale of 30 nautical miles to the inch. They feature most of Europe (except Spain and the North of Scotland). Low altitude is covered by EUR 1/2 to a scale of approximately 17 nautical miles to the inch, as far north as Edinburgh and including parts of France and Germany. Chart (EUR 3) shows the rest of Scotland.

Aerad also produce a wide range of other related documentation, including Standard Instrument Departure charts, Standard Arrival charts and airport and apron layouts. Aerad's other important publication, much prized by enthusiasts, is the Europe Supplement, a soft-backed book packed with information on airports, including their aids, runway lengths and radio frequencies.

The other chart publisher is Jeppesen Sanderson Inc, an American firm whose main distributor in the United Kingdom is CSE Aviation at Oxford Airport. Two charts cover the United Kingdom, one for high level (Ref E(HI) 3 and 4) and one for low altitudes (Ref E(LO) 1 and 2). The company also produces a variety of associated data, the most important of which are airport approach charts.

The CAA distributes a wide range of charts, many of which are of a very specialised nature. These include Aerodrome Obstruction charts, SIDs and STARs. The CAA is of course responsible for the UK Aeronautical Information Publication, known as the Air Pilot. This is really the bible for aviators in Britain's airspace but it is an extremely bulky document, divided into several volumes. Of particular interest are the AGA, COM and RAC sections, detailing aerodromes and ground aids, communications and ATC rules and procedures. It is, needless to say, very expensive and incorporates a regular updating and amendment service. All airport briefing offices have copies and you may be able to get permission to 'browse', especially if you have some *bona fide* aviation connection, such as being a flying club member.

At first sight, radio navigation charts are a perplexing welter of intersecting lines, symbols and figures, but, like any other maps, there is a key and with a few minutes' study they become logical. The radio beacons are identified by name and a three-letter abbreviation. Wallasey, for example, may be referred to by ATC and aircraft as Wallasey or Whisky Alfa Lima. The frequency of 114.1 Mhz on which the beacon radiates will be adjacent to its name on the chart. Also shown on the chart are the names of the airways, their bearings in both directions, the distances in nautical miles between reporting points, the heights of their bases and upper limits and the lowest available cruising levels.

Many of the charts are stocked by air band radio suppliers but they can also be purchased direct from the publishers or their agents at the addresses listed below. Out-of-date charts are sometimes advertised in the aviation press, often at reasonably low prices. Provided they are not too old, say more than twelve months, they can still be useful.

Suppliers of Airway Charts

British Airways, Aerad Customer Services, Bealine House, Ruislip, Middlesex HA4 6QL.

CSE Aviation Ltd (Jeppesen Agents), Oxford Airport, Kidlington, Oxford, OX5 1RA.

Royal Air Force, No 1 Aeronautical Documents Unit, RAF Northolt, West End Road, Ruislip, Middlesex HA4 6NG.

Civil Aviation Authority, Aeronautical Information Service, Tolcarne Drive, Pinner, Middlesex HA5 2DU.

Chapter 19

Magazines for the enthusiast and air band listener

In the 1960s spotters, as they were then known, relied entirely upon eyesight, sometimes aided by binoculars and telescopes. VHF receivers were commercially unavailable, even had we thought of this means of identifying some of the goodies which flew over in those days. Today, virtually every interesting aircraft movement in British skies is recorded by at least one of the enthusiast fraternity and is rapidly passed on through the grapevine. Thirty-odd years ago many questions went unanswered; was it an Armagnac I saw in 1957 heading out over the Irish Sea, did my friend really see a US Navy Tradewind and what were five Banshees (I think) doing on contrails over north-west England in 1958?

The only information available in those days on aircraft movements was published in *Air Pictorial* under the title 'Airport Notes—Interesting Visitors'. At first it was confined to Blackbushe, Croydon, Heathrow, Northolt and Prestwick and the selections, about a dozen each per month, were somewhat arbitrary. They were of little use to spotters in the Midlands and north who attempted to collate them with what they saw overhead. Gradually the net spread to embrace Manchester (Ringway as it then was), Birmingham (Elmdon), Liverpool (Speke) and other provincial airports.

Air Britain's *Movements Review*, a four-page news sheet available on subscription with other specialist publications, was much more useful and eventually local societies began to produce their own regional newsletters. One of the first in this field was the Merseyside Group of Aviation Enthusiasts which one day was to grow into the highly respected and successful Merseyside Aviation Society. For the time, quite comprehensive visitors lists were published for Speke, Ringway, Burtonwood and a few others. Among the features was a monthly 'Spotting Report', recording interesting overflights seen by members. With the advent of air band radios around 1961 the coverage spread even further, and at the same time other societies were printing their own magazines in a similar format.

Some were phenomenally detailed, even about military movements, hitherto veiled in mystery. Rumour had it that the air attachés of certain Eastern Bloc embassies had taken out subscriptions and it was said that the authorities had to have a quiet word with the editors asking them to be more discreet! Remember that security was much tighter in those days. In 1960 we were chased from the fence at Mildenhall by the air police at the spot where today there is a public enclosure! Nowadays the presence of a Lockheed U-2 at Lakenheath, which was discussed at length in the letters pages of contemporary aviation magazines without confirmation in 1956, would be known to all and sundry within hours, such is the enthusiasts' intelligence network.

Addresses for enthusiasts' magazines

Air Britain News and Air Britain Digest B. R. Womersley (Membership Secretary), 19 The Pastures, Bradford on Avon, Wiltshire BA15 2BH.

Air Strip Midland Counties Aviation Society Honorary Registrar, 113 Ferndown Road, Solihull, West Midlands B91 2AX.

Anglia Aeronews Anglian Aviation Society Administrator, 27 Eastwoodbury Lane, Southend on Sea, Essex SS2 6UY.

Aviation Letter John R. Roach, 8 Stowe Crescent, Ruislip, Middlesex HA4 7SS.

Aviation News & Review LAAS International, M. T. Reynolds, 37 Crane Close, Dagenham, Essex RM10 8PL.

British Aviation Review and Roundel British Aviation Research Group, Paul Hewins, 8 Nightingale Road, Woodley, Berkshire RG5 3LP.

Hawkeye Gatwick Aviation Society Registrar, 11 Cray Avenue, Ashtead, Surrey KT21 1QX.

Humberside Air Review Humberside Aviation Society, Pete Wild, 4 Bleach Yard, Beverley, North Humberside.

Manchester Eagle Secretary, Air Britain Manchester, 12 Fountains Road, Bramhall, Manchester.

North West Air News Air-Britain Liverpool Branch, Carl Hope, 19 Rosthwaite Road, West Derby, Liverpool L12 8QD.

Osprey Solent Aviation Society, Doreen Eaves, 84 Carnation Road, Bassett, Southampton SO2 3JL.

Prestwick Airport Letter Prestwick Airport Aviation Group, D. Reid (Editor), 45 Bellesleyhill Avenue, Ayr.

Scottish Air News Central Scotland Aviation Group, Archie McGeoch, 15 Guffock Road, Kirkconnel DG4 6QQ.

Skyward Plymouth Aircraft Research Group Honorary Secretary, 14 Dayton Close, Crownhill, Plymouth, Devon.

South East Air Review West London Aviation Group, 18 Green Lawns, Ruislip, Middlesex HA4 9SP.

Southwest Aviation News Southwest Aviation Society, Richard Hodgkinson (Registrar), Marsh Farm, Salford Priors, Near Evesham, Worcestershire.

Winged Words The Aviation Society, 64 Manchester Road, Swinton, Manchester M27 1ET.

Ulster Air Mail Ulster Aviation Society, 20 Carrowreagh Gardens, Dundonald, Belfast BT16 0TW.

Aviation Ireland Aviation Society of Ireland, 31 Shanrath Road, Whitehall, Dublin 9, Eire.

Irish Air Letter 25 Phoenix Avenue, Pecks Lane, Castleknock, Dublin 15.

Appendix 1

Beacons and reporting points

The centrelines of airways are marked by navigational beacons positioned at strategic intervals, such as where the airway changes direction or where one or more of them intersect. Airway beacons are mostly VORs with an associated DME to indicate range, but some, Lichfield being a major example, are NDBs. With the aid of a radio navigation chart it is easy to find the ones nearest to your home.

Many of the reporting points are not beacons at all, but hypothetical positions formed where certain radials from two VORs interesect, and are given a standard five-letter name. It may be related to a geographical feature such as the name of a nearby town, and is often a distortion of the real name to arrive at five letters. Examples are LAMMA on Upper Red 38 south of Edinburgh (Lammermuir Hills), SAPCO at the junction of Amber 2 and White 37 (near Sapcote in Leicestershire), and SETEL north west of Pole Hill VOR on Amber 2 (Settle). Others, particularly over the sea, are purely artificial and dreamed up by the appropriate CAA department. GRICE in Scotland, by the way, is named after a retired Supervisor at Scottish ATCC!

As described in the chapter on Approach Control, each major airport has one or more terminal beacons. Well known are the LBA at Leeds, the GM and GX at Birmingham, the CA at Castle Donington and the NEW at Newcastle. Even if the destination is not mentioned in transmissions whilst on airways, such routeings as Pole Hill-LBA will immediately give a clue. 'A standard Willo Arrival Runway 26' will identify the destination as Gatwick.

Similarly, knowledge of the runway designators at various airports will be useful. Since the trend is to a single main runway with an instrument approach aid at one or both ends, with perhaps one subsidiary for light aircraft, one can soon become familiar with those in one's home area. Examples are Birmingham 15/33, Heathrow 10L & 10R/28L & 28R, Gatwick 08/26 and Manchester 06/24.

Abbreviations used for airways in the following listings are: A = Amber, B = Blue, G = Green, R = Red, W = White. The prefix U indicates Upper and the suffixes N, S, E and W, compass points.

Beacons and reporting points used by aircraft flying the airways

Name	Code	Type	Approximate location
Aberdeen	ADN	VOR	Scottish East Coast
Ambel		RP	On UA2 near Dean Cross VOR
Amman		RP	On G1 in South Wales
Arvok		RP	Eire junction of UB2/UA38
Astra			VOR/DME holding pattern for Gatwick
Bakur		RP	Dublin/London boundary on UA38
Banba		RP	Dublin/London boundary on UB10
Barkway	BKY	VOR	
Bedfo		RP	Near Bedford on UB4
Beeno		RP	North Sea, junction of UB1/UB7
Belfast	BEL	VOR	East of Belfast city
Benbecula	BEN	VOR	Outer Hebrides
Benbo		RP	On A1 south of Worthing
Berry Head	BHD	VOR	On A25 near Torquay
Biggin	BIG	VOR	South of London. Holding pattern for Heathrow
Birmingham	GX	NDB	Birmingham Airport Northern Locator Beacon
Birmingham	GM	NDB	Birmingham Airport Southern Locator Beacon
Blaca		RP	Scotland on DG27
Blufa		RP	Amsterdam/London boundary on UB1
Blusy		RP	Amsterdam/London boundary on UB29
Bolin		RP	Holding pattern for Manchester
Bovingdon	BNN	VOR	Holding pattern for Heathrow
Bream		RP	Scottish/London boundary on UB24
Bream West		RP	Scottish/London boundary on UB24W
Brecon	BCN	VOR	South Wales on A25/G1
Bristol	BRI	NDB	Holding pattern for airport
Brookmans Park	BPK	NDB	North of London
Burnham	BUR	VOR	Berkshire

Name	Code	Type	Approximate location
Buzad		RP	SE Midlands
Calda		RP	North of Barton VOR
Carnane	CAR	NDB	Isle of Man on DG27
Chiltern	CHT	NDB	North of Heathrow
Clacton	CLN	VOR	Suffolk coast
Cliff		RP	English Channel off SE Coast
Clonmel	CML	NDB	Eire, junction of UB2/UG1
Compton	CPT	VOR	Berkshire
Congleton	CON	NDB	South of Manchester Airport
Cork	CRK	VOR	Eire
Costa	COA	VOR	Belgian coast on B29
Cowly		RP	South Midlands, junction of UW38/UA1
Crewe		RP	Cheshire, junction of UA25E/UB3
Dandi		RP	Scottish/Copenhagen boundary on UA37
Daventry	DTY	VOR	South Midlands
Dawly		RP	Off Devon coast, junction of UA25/UR8
Dayne		Offset VOR/DME	Holding pattern for Manchester and Woodford inbounds
Dean Cross	DCS	VOR	West of Carlisle
Detling	DET	VOR	Kent
Dieppe	DPE	VOR	French coast on A1E
Dogga		RP	North Sea, junction of UB1/UB13
Dover	DVR	VOR	Near town
Drake		RP	English Channel on UA34
Drumm		RP	Manchester TMA
Dublin	DUB	VOR	North of city
Dundrum		RP	South of Belfast VOR on B2
Eagle Island	EGL	VOR	North-West Eire
East Midlands	EMW	NDB	Airport holding pattern
Eastwood		VOR/DME	Holding pattern for Gatwick
Edinburgh	EDN	NDB	Nr city. Airport holding pattern
Elder		RP	Isle of Wight, junction of UR1W/UA34W
Epsom	EPM	NDB	London TMA. Holding pattern for Heathrow when Ockham VOR out of service
Evrin		RP	Dublin/London boundary on UG1

Name	Code	Type	Approximate location
Exmor	EXM	RP	North Devon, junction of UA25/UR14/UR37
Fambo		RP	North Sea on UB13
Fawbo		RP	London/France boundary on UA34W
Fawley	FAW	NDB	Near Southampton on UW38
Finch		RP	On UW22
Flamboro	FLM	RP	North Sea on UB13
Gabbard	GAB	RP	North Sea, junction of UA37/UR1N
Glasgow	GOW	VOR	Holding pattern for Glasgow
Glesk		RP	South of Aberdeen on B22
Goodwood	GWD	VOR	South Coast on UR25
Grice		RP	Northern extremity of Scottish TMA
Guernsey	GUR	VOR	On UR1
Hardy		RP	South of Seaford on A1
Hasty		RP	On W8
Hazel		RP	Southern England, junction of UR8/UR1W
Honiley	HON	VOR	South of Birmingham airport
Ibsley	IBY	VOR	Southern England, junction UR8/UR14
Inverness	INS	VOR	North East Scotland
Isle of Man	IOM	VOR	Southern tip of island
Jersey	JEY	NDB	Near Jersey Airport
Kathy		RP	English Channel, junction of UR1/UA34W
Kenet		RP	On G1 east of Lyneham NDB
Killiney	KLY	NDB	Near Dublin, on junction of UB2/UR14
Koksy	KOK	VOR	Belgian coast on G1
Konan		RP	Amsterdam/London boundary on UG1
Lambourne	LAM	VOR	North of London. Holding pattern for Heathrow
Lands End	LND	VOR	Lands End
Lamma		RP	South of Edinburgh on UR38
Largs		RP	Ayrshire coast on B2
Leeck		RP	South of Congleton NDB
Leeds	LBA	NDB	Near airport. Holding pattern
Lichfield	LIC	NDB	Midlands, junction of A1E/W37
Liffy	LFY	RP	London/Dublin boundary on UB1

Name	Code	Type	Approximate location
Liverpool	LPL	NDB	Holding pattern for airport
Lizad		RP	France/London boundary on UG4
Longsand	LSD	RP	Junction of UB29/UR1S/UA37
Luton	LUT	NDB	Holding point for airport
Lylak		R	Holding pattern for Manchester
Lynas		RP	Anglesey on B1
Lyneham	LA	NDB	Wiltshire
Mable		RP	South of Belfast VOR on R3
Macrihanish	MAC	VOR	Kintyre, Scotland
Malby		RP	On G1 between Brecon and Kenet
Manchester	MCT	VOR	On the airport
Margo		RP	South Scotland
Mayfield	MAY	VOR	Sussex, junction of W17/A34E/A30
Merly		RP	Bristol Channel, junction UB40/UR37
Midhurst	MID	VOR	Sussex
Nevil		RP	London/Brest boundary on W8
Newcastle	NEW	VOR	North east coast. Holding pattern for Newcastle airport
New Galloway	NGY	NDB	South Scotland
Norla		RP	Dublin/London boundary on UR37
Norry		RP	South Midlands
Ockham	OCK	VOR	London TMA. Holding pattern for Heathrow
Ortac		RP	France/London boundary on UR1/UR14
Orton		RP	North of Pole Hill VOR
Ottringham	OTR	VOR	Humberside on B1
Parka		RP	Liverpool Bay on R3
Patch		RP	North Sea, junction UR4/UB24
Pole Hill	POL	VOR	North of Manchester on A1
Prestwick	PWK	VOR	On airport. Holding pattern
Radno		RP	South Wales on W39
Redfa		RP	London/Amsterdam boundary on R1N
Reeky		RP	Near Edinburgh
Rexam		RP	Wrexham on A25
Robin		RP	North Midlands
St Abbs Head	SAB	VOR	Scottish East Coast on UR23
Salco		RP	France/London boundary on UR1

Name	Code	Type	Approximate location
Sandy		RP	South Coast on A2
Sapco		RP	North Midlands, junction of A2/W37
Seaford	SFD	VOR	South Coast on UA2
Setel		RP	North west of Pole Hill VOR
Shannon	SNN	VOR	South west Eire
Sitet		RP	France/London boundary on UA34
Skery		RP	South of Berry Head VOR on A25
Skeso		RP	France/London boundary on UA25
Skipness	SKP	VOR	West Scotland
Slany		RP	Dublin/London boundary on G1
Southampton	SAM	VOR	On the airport
Stafford	STF	RP	North Midlands
Stansted	SAN	NDB	Holding pattern for airport
Stornoway	STN	VOR	Outer Hebrides
Strumble	STU	VOR	Coast of SW Wales
Swany		RP	Bristol Channel on UB40
Talla	TLA	VOR	South Scotland
Tawny		VOR/DME	Holding pattern for Heathrow when Lambourne VOR out of service
Telba		RP	South of Crewe, junction of UA25E/UA34
Tivli		RP	Dublin/London boundary on UG4
Tolka		RP	Dublin/London boundary on UW39
Trent	TNT	VOR	North Midlands
Tripo		RP	On R15
Upton		RP	On B1 east of Barton VOR
Vatry		RP	Dublin/London boundary on UR14
Venom		RP	Manchester Zone
Wallasey	WAL	VOR	Wirral Peninsula
Weald		VOR/DME	holding pattern for Heathrow when Biggin VOR out of service
Wescott	WCO	NDB	South Midlands
Whitegate	WHI	NDB	Manchester TMA SW boundary

Name	Code	Type	Approximate location
Wick	WIK	VOR	Northern Scotland
Willo		VOR/DME	holding pattern for Gatwick
Wizad		RP	West of Dover on W17
Wobun		RP	South Midlands
Woodley	WOD	NDB	Southern England, junction of G1/A1E
Worthing	WOR	RP	English Channel on UA1

Appendix 2

Airways frequency allocation

AIRWAYS

	AREA	**CALLSIGN**	**FREQ**	**REMARKS (Freq as Directed)**
A1	Skipness - Prestwick	*Scottish Control*	124.9	
	Prestwick - N54 30	*Scottish Control*	{126.25 124.9	
	N54 30 - Abm Stafford			
	above FL155	*London Control*	131.05	129.1, 134.425
	at or below FL155	*Manchester Control*	126.65	124.2
	Abm Stafford-Birmingham			
	above FL135	*London Control*	133.7	134.425
	at or below FL135	*Manchester Control*	124.2 †	
	Birmingham - Abm Woodley	*London Control*	133.7 †	126.825
	S of Woodley - FIR Bdry	*London Control*	127.7	124.275
A1E	Pole Hill - Lichfield			
	above FL155	*London Control*	131.05	
	at or below FL155	*Manchester Control*	126.65	124.2
	Lichfield - Abm Birmingham			
	above FL135	*London Control*	133.7	
	at or below FL135	*Manchester Control*	124.2	
	Abm Birmingham - Woodley	*London Control*	133.7	134.75, 126.825
	S of Woodley - Fir Bdry	*London Control*	127.7	135.050, 124.275
A2	Between Talla and N54 30	*Scottish Control*	128.5 124.9	
	Between N54 30 and Abm Lichfield			
	above FL155	*London Control*	131.05	134.425
	at or below FL155	*Manchester Control*	126.65	124.20
	Between Abm Lichfield and Abm Birmingham			
	above FL135	*London Control*	134.75	133.7, 134.425
	at or below 135	*Manchester Control*	124.20	
	Between Amb Birmingham and Brookmans Park	*London Control*	134.75	133.7, 126.825
	South of Brookmans Park to FIR bdy	*London Control*	127.1	132.45
A2W	Within London FIR	*London Control*	127.1	
A25	Dean Cross - N54 30	*Scottish Control*	{126.25 124.9	
	N54 30 - Rexham			
	above FL155	*London Control*	128.05	129.1, 134.425

	AREA	CALLSIGN	FREQ	REMARKS (Freq as Directed)
	at or below FL155	*Manchester Control*	133.05	125.1
	Rexham - Cardiff	*London Control*	131.2	
	Cardiff - N50 00	*London Control*	132.6	135.25
	N50 00 - Southern Boundary of Channel Islands Zone	*Jersey Zone*	125.2	
A30	Within London FIR	*London Control*	127.1	
A34	Within London FIR	*London Control*	127.7	124.275
A34E	Within London FIR	*London Control*	127.7	124.275
A37	Entire Airway	*London Control*	129.6	127.95, 133.45, 133.525
B1	W of Wallasey			
	above FL135	*London Control*	128.05	129.1, 134.425
	at or below FL135	*Manchester Control*	133.05	
	Wallasey - Barton			
	above FL155	*London Control*	128.05	134.425
	at or below FL155	*Manchester Control*	125.1	
	Barton - Ottringham			
	above FL155	*London Control*	131.05	134.425
	at or below FL155	*Manchester Control*	126.65	124.2
	E of Ottringham	*London Control*	134.25	127.95, 133.525
B2	East of Glasgow	*Scottish Control*	128.5	
	Glasgow - FIR Bdry	*Scottish Control*	124.9	
B3	Wallasey - Stafford			
	above FL155	*London Control*	128.05	129.1
	at or below FL155	*Manchester Control*	125.1	124.2
	Stafford - Abm Birmingham			
	above FL135	*London Control*	133.7 †	134.75
	at or below FL135	*Manchester Control*	125.1 †	124.2
	Abm Birmingham - Brookmans Park	*London Control*	133.7 †	134.75, 126.825
	S of Brookmans Park - FIR Bdry	*London Control*	127.1	134.9
B4	Detling - Brookmans Park	*London Control*	127.1	134.9
	Brookmans Park - Abm Birmingham	*London Control*	134.75	133.7, 126.825
	Abm Birmingham - Robin			
	above FL135	*London Control*	134.75	133.7, 134.425
	at or below FL135	*Manchester Control*	124.2	126.65
	Robin - Pole Hill			
	above FL155	*London Control*	131.05	134.425
	at or below FL155	*Manchester Control*	124.2	126.65
	Pole hill - N54 30			
	above FL155	*London Control*	131.05	134.425
	at or below FL155	*Manchester Control*	126.65	124.2
	N54 30 - Grice	*Scottish Control*	128.5 124.9	
B11	Within London FIR	*London Control*	134.45	127.7, 124.275
B22	Entire Route	*Scottish Control*	124.5	
B29	Within London FIR	*London Control*	129.6	127.95
G1	West of Brecon	*London Control*	131.2	
	Brecon - Abm Woodley	*London Control*	132.8	131.2
	East of Abm Woodley to FIR Bdry	*London Control*	134.9	127.1
R1	Entire route	*London Control*	134.45	127.7, 132.3, 124.275

	AREA	CALLSIGN	FREQ	REMARKS (Freq as Directed)
R1N	Within London FIR	*London Control*	129.6	127.95, 133.45, 133.525
R1W	Entire route	*London Control*	134.45	132.3, 127.7, 124.275
R1S	Within London FIR	*London Control*	129.6	127.95, 133.45, 133.525
R3	W of Belfast	*Scottish Control*	124.9	
	Belfast - Wallasey			
	above FL135	*London Control*	128.05	129.1, 134.425
	at or below FL135	*Manchester Control*	133.05	125.1
	Wallasey - Robin			
	above FL155	*London Control*	128.05	129.1, 134.425
	at or below FL155	*Manchester Control*	125.1	124.2
R14	Within London FIR	*London Control*	131.2	
R23	Entire Route	*Scottish Control*	124.9	126.250, 128.5
R25	Entire Route	*London Control*	127.7	
W7	Entire Airway	*London Control*	127.7	124.275
W8	North of N50 00	*London Control*	127.7	124.275
W17	N50 00 - Midhurst	*London Control*	134.45	132.3, 127.7, 124.275
	Midhurst - Dover	*London Control*	134.9	127.1, 124.275
W22	Biggin - Abm Birmingham	*London Control*	134.75	133.7, 126.825
	Abm Birmingham - Pole Hill			
	above FL155	*London Control*	131.05	
	at or below FL155	*Manchester Control*	124.2	126.65
W23	Entire Route			
	above FL155	*London Control*	131.05	129.1, 134.425
	at or below FL155	*Manchester Control*	126.65	124.2
W37	Entire Route			
	above FL155	*London Control*	128.05	129.1
	at or below FL155	*Manchester Control*	125.1	124.2
W38	Ortac - Sam	*London Control*	134.45	132.3, 127.7, 124.275
	Sam - Abm Compton	*London Control*	132.8	131.2, 124.275
	Abm Compton - Westcott	*London Control*	133.7	134.75
W39	Malby - Radno	*London Control*	131.2	
	Radno - Tolka	*London Control*	128.05	

†Birmingham Zone Control freq 120.5 is delegated Controlling Authority for Daventry Control Area airspace within Airway *A1* co-incident with the boundaries of Birmingham SRA/SRZ up to and including FL80.

UPPER ATS ROUTES

	AREA	CALLSIGN	FREQ	REMARKS (Freq as Directed)
UA1	North of N54 30	*Scottish Control*	135.85	
	N54 30 - Abm Lichfield	*London Control*	131.05	129.1, 134.425
	Abm Lichfield - Abm Woodley	*London Control*	133.7	
	South of Woodley - UIR Bdry	*London Control*	127.7	124.275
UA1E	Daventry - Woodley	*London Control*	133.7	134.75
	South of Woodley - UIR Bdry	*London Control*	127.7	135.05
UA2	Dean Cross - N54 30	*Scottish Control*	135.85	
	N54 30 - Trent	*London Control*	131.05	129.1, 134.425
	Trent - Brookmans Park	*London Control*	133.7	134.75
	South of Brookmans Park - UIR Bdry	*London Control*	127.1	132.45
UA2W	Entire route	*London Control*	127.1	

	AREA	CALLSIGN	FREQ	REMARKS (Freq as Directed)
UA25	Dean Cross - N54 30	*Scottish Control*	135.85	
	N54 30 - South of Wallasey	*London Control*	128.05	129.1, 134.425
	South of Wallasey - South of Brecon	*London Control*	133.6	
	South of Brecon - UIR Bdry	*London Control*	132.6	131.05, 134.425
UA25E	Pole Hill - Telba	*London Control*	131.05	129.1
	Telba - Exmor	*London Control*	133.6	
UA30	Entire route	*London Control*	127.1	
UA34	Wallasey - Telba	*London Control*	128.05	129.1
	Telba - Abm Woodley	*London Control*	133.7	
	Abm Woodley - UIR Bdry	*London Control*	127.7	124.275
UA37	Dandi - Gabbard	*London Control*	134.25	128.125, 133.525
	Gabbard - Detling	*London Control*	129.6	127.95, 133.525
UA38	Within London UIR	*London Control*	133.6	
UB1	West of Wallasey	*London Control*	128.05	134.425
	Wallasey - Ottringham	*London Control*	131.05	134.425
	East of Ottringham	*London Control*	134.25	128.125, 133.525
UB3	North of N53 00	*London Control*	128.05	
	N53 00 - Brookmans Park	*London Control*	133.7	134.75
	Brookmans Park - Dover	*London Control*	127.1, 134.9	
UB4	Perth - N54 30	*Scottish Control*	135.85	
	N54 30 - Robin	*London Control*	131.05	134.425
	Robin - Brookmans Park	*London Control*	134.75	133.7
	S of Brookmans Park - UIR Bdy	*London Control*	127.1	132.45
UB10	Within London UIR	*London Control*	133.6	
UB11	Within the London UIR	*London Control*	134.45	127.7, 124.275
*UB13**	North of Fambo	*Scottish Control*	135.85	
	South of Fambo	*London Control*	134.25	128.125, 134.525
*UB22**	Entire Route	*Scottish Control*	135.85	124.05
*UB24**	N of Bream	*Scottish Control*	135.85	124.05
	S of Bream	*London Control*	134.25	128.125
UB24W	N of Bream West	*Scottish Control*	135.85	124.05
	S of Bream West	*London Control*	134.25	128.125
UB29	Abm Woodley - Abm Brookmans Park	*London Control*	129.6	127.95, 133.525
	East of Abm Brookmans Park - UIR Boundary	*London Control*	129.6	127.95
UB40	Entire route	*London Control*	133.6	132.6
UB42	Within London UIR	*London Control*	132.60	
UB427	Strumble - Lundy	*London Control*	133.6	
	Lundy - Berry Head	*London Control*	132.6	
UG1	West of Abm Woodley - UIR boundary	*London Control*	133.6	132.8
	East of Abm Woodley - UIR boundary	*London Control*	134.9	127.1
UG4	Within London UIR	*London Control*	132.6	
UG11	Within Scottish UIR	*Scottish Control*	135.85	124.05
UL1	W of Abm Woodley - UIR boundary	*London Control*	133.6	132.8
	E of Abm Woodley - UIR boundary	*London Control*	134.9	127.1
UL7	North of Skate	*Scottish Control*	135.85	124.05

	AREA	CALLSIGN	FREQ	REMARKS (Freq as Directed)
	South of Skate	*London Control*	134.25	128.125
UR1	West of or abm Lambourne	*London Control*	134.45	127.7, 132.3, 124.275
UR1N } *UR1S* }	East of or abm Lambourne - UIR boundary	*London Control*	129.6	127.95, 133.45, 133.525
UR1W	Entire Route	*London Control*	132.3	127.7
*UR3**	Entire Route	*London Control*	128.05	134.425
UR4	W of Pole Hill	*London Control*	128.05	134.425
	Pole Hill - Ottringham	*London Control*	131.05	134.425
	E of Ottringham	*London Control*	134.25	128.125, 133.525
UR8	N50 00 W008 00 - Samtn	*London Control*	134.45	132.3, 127.7, 124.275
	Samtn - Midhurst	*London Control*	134.45	132.3, 127.7, 124.275
UR8S	Entire Route	*London Control*	132.6	
UR14	Within London UIR	*London Control*	132.6	133.6
UR16N	Within London UIR	*London Control*	132.6	
	Within Scottish UIR	*Scottish Control*	135.85	
*UR23**	Within Scottish UIR	*Scottish Control*	135.85	
UR25	Entire Route	*London Control*	127.7	124.275
UR37	West of Samtn	*London Control*	132.6	124.275
	Samtn - abm Midhurst	*London Control*	134.45	127.7, 132.3, 124.275
	East of abm Midhurst	*London Control*	134.9	127.1, 124.275
UR38	Entire Route	*Scottish Control*	135.85	124.05
UR72	Within London UR	*London Control*	132.60	
UW14	Entire Route	*Scottish Control*	135.85	
UW24	Orist - Aspen	*London Control*	134.45	132.3, 127.7
UW38	Ortac - Samtn	*London Control*	134.45	132.3, 1277
	Samtn - abm Woodley	*London Control*	132.8	131.2
	Woodley - Westcott	*London Control*	134.75, 133.7	
UW39	Midhurst - Radno	*London Control*	133.6	132.6
	Radno - Tolka	*London Control*	128.05	

*On these UPPER ATS ROUTES, or portions thereof, ATC radar service is normally provided to all co-operating civil and military aircraft and is co-ordinated at the Joint Air Traffic Control Radar Units (JATCRU). Aircraft will normally be instructed by London or Scottish ATCCs to communicate directly with one of the following JATCRUs:-

BOULMER: Callsign *Border Radar* on 134.85
BUCHAN: Callsign *Highland Radar* on 134.1

LOWER ATS ADVISORY ROUTES

	AREA	CALLSIGN	FREQ	REMARKS (Freq as Directed)
DA1	Within the Scottish FIR	*Scottish Control*	124.9†	
DB22	Within the Scottish FIR	*Scottish Control*	131.3 / 133.2	
DG4	Within the London FIR	*London Control*	132.6	
DG27W	North of BLACA	*Scottish Control*	126.65 / 124.9	
	South of BLACA			
	above FL135	*London Control*	128.05	129.1, 134.425
	at or below FL135	*Manchester Control*	133.05	
DG27E	W of North Light			
	above FL135	*London Control*	128.05	129.1, 134.425
	at or below FL135	*Manchester Control*	133.05	

	AREA	CALLSIGN	FREQ	REMARKS (Freq as Directed)
	E of North Light			
	above FL155	*London Control*	128.05	134.425
	at or below FL155	*Manchester Control*	133.05	
DR8	Within London FIR	*London Control*	132.6	
DR37	Within London FIR	*London Control*	132.6	
DW2	W of Fleetwood			
	above FL135	*London Control*	128.05	129.1, 134.425
	at or below FL135	*Manchester Control*	133.05	
	E of Fleetwood			
	above FL155	*London Control*	131.05	134.425
	at or below FL155	*Manchester Control*	126.65	124.2
DW3	S of Inverness	*Scottish Control*	124.5	
	Inverness - Sumburgh	*Scottish Control*	{131.3 / 133.2}	
DW4	Within Scottish FIR	*Scottish Control*	{131.3 / 133.2}	
DW5	Within Scottish FIR	*Scottish Control*	{131.3 / 133.2}	
DW6	Glasgow - Stornoway	*Scottish Control*	124.9	
	Stornoway - Inverness	*Scottish Control*	{131.3 / 133.2}	
DW10	Within the Scottish FIR	*Scottish Control*	124.9	
DW11	E of B4	*Scottish Control*	128.5††	
	W of B4			
	above FL135	*London Control*	128.05	129.1, 134.425
	at or below FL135	*Manchester Control*	133.05	
DW55	Within Scottish FIR	*Scottish Control*	124.9	
DW56	Entire Route	*Scottish Control*	124.9	
DW57	Entire Route	*Scottish Control*	124.9	
DW58	Entire Route	*Scottish Control*	124.9	

****NORTHERN JOINT RADAR ADVISORY SERVICE AREA**

Entire Area	Border Radar	132.9

** Outside published Op hrs, FIS aval from London ATCC on 134.7 and Mil MAS Service from Border Radar (Mil) on 228.5.

† Acft at lower levels between Stornoway and W010 00 unable to communicate on 124.9 should use 131.3.

†† Communications will be with *Border Radar* on freq 132.9 during the hours of operation of Border Radar.

CONTROL AREAS

NAME	AREA	CALLSIGN	FREQ
*HEBRIDES UPPER	Entire area	*Scottish Control*	135.85

*South of a line from N57 00 W10 00 to Skipness and West of a line from Skipness to Belfast, between◇0400 and 1800, use 126.85.

ndix 3

VHF air band frequencies

Frequencies of airports and airfields

Aberdeen: Tower: 121.7 GMC: 121.7 Approach: 120.4 Radar: 121.25/128.3 ATIS: 121.85
Abingdon: Tower: 130.25 Also see Benson
Aberporth: AFIS: 122.15
Alderney: Tower: 123.6
Alicante: Tower: 118.1 GMC: 121.7 Approach: 118.8
Amsterdam: Tower: 118.1 GMC: 121.8 Approach: 121.2/131.15/119.05
Andrews Field: A/G: 130.55
Audley End: A/G: 122.35 (By arrangement)
Barcelona: Tower: 118.1 GMC: 121.7 Approach: 119.1/124.7
Barrow: A/G: (Walney Island) 123.2
Barton: A/G: 122.7
Bedford: Tower: 130.0 Approach: 130.7 Radar: 124.2
Belfast (Aldergrove): Tower: 118.3 Approach: 120.0 Radar: 120.9
Belfast Harbour: Tower: 130.75 Approach: 130.85 Radar: 122.45
Bembridge, Isle of Wight: A/G: 123.25
Benbecula: Tower/Approach: 119.2
Benson: Tower: 122.1 Approach: 120.9 MATZ
Biggin Hill: Tower: 134.8 Approach: 129.4
Binbrook: Binbrook Zone 125.35
Birmingham: Tower: 118.3 GMC: 121.8 Approach: 120.5 Radar: 118.05
Blackbushe: AFIS: 122.3
Blackpool: Tower: 118.4 Approach: 135.95 Radar: 119.95
Bodmin: A/G: 122.7
Booker (Wycombe Air Park): AFIS: 126.55 GMC: 121.6
Border Radar: 132.9 134.85
Boscombe Down: Tower: 130.0 Approach: 125.35 Radar: 130.75
Bourn: A/G: 129.8
Bournemouth (Hurn): Tower: 125.6 Approach: 118.65 Radar: 119.75 ATIS: 121.95
Brawdy: MATZ 124.4
Bridlington: A/G: 123.24

Bristol (Filton): Tower: 124.95 Approach: 130.85
Bristol (Lulsgate): Tower: 120.55 Approach: 127.75 Radar: 124.35
Brize Norton: Radar: 134.3/119.0
Brough: Tower: 130.55 Approach: 118.25
Brussels: Tower: 118.6 GMC: 121.875 Approach: 118.25/122.5/127.15
Caernarfon: A/G: 122.25
Cambridge: Tower: 122.2 Approach: 123.6 Radar: 130.75
Cardiff: Tower: 121.2 Approach: 124.85 Radar: 120.05
Carlisle: Tower/Approach: 123.6
Chivenor: MATZ: 130.20
Chichester (Goodwood): Tower: 120.65 Approach: 122.45
Church Fenton: Tower: 122.10 Approach: 126.5
Coltishall: MATZ: 125.9
Compton Abbas: A/G: 122.7
Coningsby: MATZ & Approach: 120.80
Copenhagen: Tower: 118.1/119.9 GMC: 121.9 Approach: 119.8/119.35/120.25
Cottesmore: MATZ: 130.2
Coventry: Tower/Approach: 119.25 Radar: 122.0
Cranfield: Tower: 123.2 Approach/Radar: 122.85
Cranwell: MATZ: 119.0
Culdrose: Tower: 122.1 Approach: 130.05 Radar: 123.3
Denham: A/G: 130.725
Doncaster: A/G: 122.9
Dounreay (Thurso): Tower/Approach: 122.4
Dublin: Tower: 118.6 GMC: 121.8 Approach: 121.1/119.55/118.5
Dundee: Tower/Approach: 122.9
Dunsfold: Tower: 124.325 Approach: 122.55 Radar: 122.55/118.825
Dunkeswell: A/G: 123.5
Duxford: AFIS/A/G: 123.5
Earls Colne A/G: 122.425
Eastern Radar (Watton): 134.3
East Midlands/Castle Donington: Tower: 124.0 GMC: 121.9 Approach: 119.65 Radar: 120.15
Edinburgh: Tower: 118.7 GMC: 121.75 Approach: 121.2 Radar: 124.25
Elstree: A/G: 122.4
Enniskillen: (St. Angelo) A/G: 123.2
Enstone A/G: 129.875
Exeter: Tower: 119.8 Approach: 128.15 Radar: 119.05
Fairford: Tower: 119.0 See Brize Norton
Fairoaks: A/G: 123.425
Falmouth Radar: 122.1
Farnborough: Tower: 122.5 Approach: 134.35 Radar: 130.05 Zone: 125.25
Fenland: AFIS/A/G: 123.05
Finningley: Tower: 122.1 Approach: 120.35 Radar: 123.3
Flotta: A/G: 122.15

Ford: A/G: 122.0
Frankfurt: Tower: 119.9 GMC: 121.9 Approach: 120.8/120.15/119.15
Geneva: Tower: 118.7 GMC: 121.9 Approach: 120.3/130.15/121.3
Glasgow: Tower: 118.8 GMC: 121.7 Approach: 119.1 Radar: 119.3/121.3
Glenrothes: A/G: 130.45
Gloucester/Cheltenham Staverton: Tower/Approach: 125.65 Radar: 122.9
Great Yarmouth (North Denes): A/G: 120.45
Guernsey: Tower: 119.95 Approach: 128.65 Radar: 118.9/124.5
Halfpenny Green: GMC: 121.95 AFIS: 123.0
Hatfield: Tower: 130.8 Approach/Radar: 123.35 Radar: 119.3
Haverfordwest: A/G: 122.2
Hawarden: Tower: 124.95 Approach: 123.35 Radar: 129.85
Highland Radar: 134.1 126.1 134.3
Honington: MATZ: 129.05 (Common frequency for Mildenhall and Lakenheath)
Hucknall: A/G: 130.8
Humberside: Tower: 118.55 Approach: 123.15 121.775
Inverness (Dalcross): Tower/Approach: 122.6
Ipswich: Tower/Approach: 118.325
Islay (Port Ellen): AFIS: 123.15
Isle of Man (Ronaldsway): Tower: 118.9 Approach/Radar: 120.85/118.2/125.3
Isle of Wight (Sandown): A/G: 123.5
Jersey: Tower: 119.45 GMC: 121.9 Approach: 120.3 Radar: 118.55/120.3 Zone: 125.2/120.45
Kemble: MATZ: 122.1
Kent Radar: 129.45
Kinloss: Tower: 122.1 Approach: 119.35 Radar: 123.3/118.9
Kirkwall: Tower/Approach: 118.3
Lakenheath: MATZ 129.05
Lands End (St Just): A/G: 122.3
Lashenden (Headcorn): A/G: 122.0
Leavesden: Tower/Approach: 122.15 Radar: 121.4
Leeds–Bradford: Tower: 120.3 Approach: 123.75 Radar: 121.05
Leeming: Tower: 122.1 MATZ Approach Radar: 132.4
Lee-on-Solent: Tower: 135.7 Approach: 133.55
Leicester: AFIS/A/G/: 122.25
Lerwick (Tingwall): A/G: 122.6
Leuchars: Tower: 122.1 Approach: 126.5 Radar: 123.3
Linton-on-Ouse: MATZ: 129.15
Little Snoring: A/G: 122.4
Liverpool: Tower: 118.1 Approach/Radar: 119.85 Radar: 118.45
Llanbedr: Radar: 122.5
London Gatwick: Tower: 124.225 GMC: 121.95/121.8 Approach: 119.6 Radar: 125.875/118.6 ATIS: 121.75/117.9 GMP: 121.95
London Heathrow: Tower: 118.7/118.5 GMC: 121.9/121.7 Approach: 119.2/

~~120.4~~/119.5/127.55 Radar: 119.9 ATIS: 121.85/133.075 120.4
London Stansted: Tower: 118.15 Approach: 125.55 Radar: 126.95/123.8
London (Westland Heliport): Battersea Tower: 122.9
Londonderry (Eglinton): Tower/Approach: 122.85
Lossiemouth: Tower: 123.3 Approach: 119.35 Radar: 123.3
Luton: Tower: 120.2 GMC: 121.75 Approach: 129.55/128.75 Radar: 127.3
Lydd: Approach: 120.7 Radar: 131.3
Lyneham: Tower: 123.4 Approach: 123.4/118.425 Radar: 123.3
Machrihanish: Tower: 122.1 Approach: 122.1/125.9 Radar: 123.3
Madrid: Tower: 118.15 GMC: 121.7 Approach: 119.9/120.9/139.5
Malaga: Tower: 118.15/139.3 GMC: 121.7 Approach: 118.45/119.3
Manchester International: Tower: 118.7 Approach: 119.4 Radar: 121.35 GMC: 121.7 ATIS: 128.175
Manston: Tower: 124.9/122.1 Approach: 126.35/123.0
Marham: Tower: 122.1 Approach: 124.15 Radar: 123.3
Midland Radar (North Luffenham): 132.25
Mildenhall: Tower: 122.55 Approach: 129.05 Radar: 123.3
Netherthorpe: A/G: 123.5
Newcastle: Tower: 119.7 Approach: 126.35 Radar: 118.5
Newtonards: A/G: 123.5
Northampton (Sywell): AFIS/A/G: 122.7
Northolt: Tower: ~~134.15~~ Approach: ~~134.15~~ Radar: 120.35/123.3 TWR/APP. 126.45
Norwich: Tower: 118.9 Approach: 119.35 Radar: 124.25
Nottingham: A/G: 122.8
Old Warden (Shuttleworth Collection): 123.05
Ostend: Tower: 118.7 GMC: 121.9 Approach 120.6
Oxford: Tower: 119.8 Approach: 130.3 GMC: 121.75 ATIS: 121.95
Pailton (Rugby): Radio Test Centre 126.05 (By arrangement)
Palma: Tower: 118.3/139.3 GMC: 121.7 Approach: 119.4/119.15/118.95
Panshanger: A/G: 120.25
Paris (Charles de Gaulle): Tower: 119.25 GMC: 121.6/126.65 Approach: 121.15/119.85/118.15
Paris (Le Bourget): Tower: 119.1 GMC: 121.9 Approach: 121.15/119.85/118.15
Paris (Orly): Tower: 118.7/121.05 GMC: 121.7 Approach: 120.85/118.85/124.45
Paull: A/G: 123.0
Penzance Heliport: A/G: 118.1
Perth (Scone): Tower: 119.8 Approach: 122.3
Pershore: MATZ: 120.8
Peterborough (Conington): A/G: 123.0
Peterborough (Sibson): A/G: 122.3
Plymouth (Roborough): Tower: 122.6 Approach: 123.2
Popham: A/G: 129.8
Portland Radar: 124.15

Prestwick: Tower: 118.15 Approach: 120.55 Radar: 119.45
Redhill: AFIS: 123.225
Retford/Gamston: A/G: 130.475
Rochester: AFIS: 122.25
Rome (Fiumicino): Tower: 118.7/119.3 GMC: 121.9 Approach: 119.2
St Mawgan: Tower: 123.4 Approach: 126.5 Radar: 125.55/123.3
Samlesbury: Tower: 130.35 Approach (Warton): 124.45
Sandtoft: A/G: 130.425
Scatsta: Tower/Approach: 123.6 Radar: 122.4
Scilly Isles: Tower: 123.15
Seething: A/G: 122.6
Shannon: Tower: 118.7 GMC: 121.8 Approach: 121.4/120.2
Shawbury: Tower: 122.10 Approach: 124.15
Sherburn-in-Elmet: A/G: 122.6
Shetland Radar: 118.15
Shipdham: A/G: 123.05
Shobdon: A/G: 123.5
Shoreham: Tower: 125.4 Approach: 123.15
Skegness: A/G: 130.45
Sleap: A/G: 122.45
Silverstone: A/G: 122.7 (race days only)
Southampton: Tower: 118.2 Approach: 128.85 Zone: 121.3/131.0
Southend: Tower: 119.7 Approach: 128.95 Radar: 129.45/125.05
Skegness: A/G: 130.45
Stapleford Tawney: AFIS/A/G: 122.8
Stornoway: Tower/Approach: 123.5
Sturgate: A/G: 130.3
Sumburgh: Tower: 118.25 Approach: 123.15 Radar: 119.25/130.05 ATIS 125.85
Swansea: Tower/Approach: 119.7 Radar: 120.75
Strubby Heliport, Lincolnshire: A/G: 122.375
Tatenhill: A/G: 122.2
Teeside: Tower: 119.8 Approach: 118.85 Radar: 128.85
Thruxton: A/G: 130.45
Tiree: AFIS: 122.7
Unst: Tower/Approach: 130.35
Upper Heyford: MATZ: 128.55
Valley: Tower: 122.1 Approach: 134.35
Waddington: Tower 127.35 Approach: 127.35 Radar: 123.3
Warton: Tower: 130.8 Approach: 124.45
Wattisham: Tower: 122.1 Approach: 123.4 Radar: 123.3
Wellesbourne Mountford: A/G: 130.45
West Freugh: Tower: 122.55 Approach/Radar: 130.05
Weston Super Mare: Tower: 122.5 Approach: 129.25
Wethersfield: Tower: 122.1 MATZ: 123.4

White Waltham: A/G: 122.6
Wick: Tower/Approach 119.7
Wickenby: A/G: 122.45
Wittering: MATZ: 130.2 (Cottesmore)
Woodford: Tower: 126.925 Approach: 130.05 Radar: 130.75
Wycombe Airpark (Booker): A/G: 126.55 121.6
Wyton: MATZ: 134.05
Yeovil (Judwin): Tower: 125.4 Approach: 130.8
Yeovilton: MATZ: 127.35
Zurich: Tower: 118.1/119.7 GMC: 121.9 Approach: 118.0/120.75/119.7/125.95/127.75

Airband frequencies in numerical order

MHz

117.9	Gatwick ATIS
118.00	Greenham Common Radar
118.05	Birmingham Radar
118.10	Liverpool Tower/Aberdeen Tower/Penzance Heliport/Scilly Isles
118.15	Prestwick Tower/Stansted Tower/Shetland Radar
118.20	Ronaldsway Radar/Southampton Tower
118.25	Sumburgh Tower/Brough Approach
118.30	Birmingham Tower/Belfast (Aldergrove) Tower/Kirkwall Tower/Approach
118.325	Ipswich Tower & Approach
118.35	
118.40	Blackpool Tower
118.45	Liverpool Radar
118.425	Biggin Hill AFIS/Lyneham Approach
> 118.50	Heathrow Tower/Newcastle Radar/Dublin Radar
118.55	Jersey Tower/Humberside Tower
118.60	Gatwick Radar/Dublin Tower
118.65	Hurn Approach
> 118.70	Edinburgh Tower/Heathrow Tower/Manchester Tower/Shannon Tower
118.75	
118.80	Glasgow Tower/Cork Radar
118.825	Dunsfold Radar
118.85	Teeside Approach
118.90	Guernsey Radar/Isle of Man Tower/Norwich Tower
118.95	Gatwick Radar
119.00	RAF Common Frequency
119.05	Exeter Radar
119.10	Glasgow Approach
119.15	

119.20	Heathrow Approach/Benbecula Tower
119.25	Coventry Tower/Sumburgh Radar
119.30	Cork Tower/Hatfield Radar
119.35	Lossiemouth Approach/Norwich Approach
119.40	Manchester Approach
119.45	Jersey Tower/Prestwick Radar
119.50	Heathrow Approach
119.55	Dublin Radar
119.60	Gatwick Approach/Prestwick Approach
119.65	Castledon Approach
119.70	Swansea Tower/Approach/Southend Tower/Wick Tower/ Newcastle Tower
119.75	Hurn Radar
119.80	Exeter Tower/Oxford Tower/Perth Tower/Teeside Tower
119.85	Liverpool Approach/Radar
119.90	Heathrow Radar/Cork Approach
119.95	Blackpool Radar/Guernsey Tower
120.00	Belfast (Aldergrove) Approach
120.05	Cardiff Radar
120.10	
120.15	Castledon Radar
120.20	Luton Tower/Shannon Approach
120.25	Panshanger A/G
120.30	Jersey Approach/Leeds Tower
120.35	Finningley Radar
120.40	Aberdeen Approach/Heathrow Radar
120.45	Jersey Zone/North Denes
120.50	Birmingham Approach
120.55	Bristol (Lulsgate) Tower/Prestwick Approach
120.60	
120.65	Woodvale Tower/Goodwood Tower
120.70	Lydd Approach
120.75	Swansea Radar
120.80	Coningsby Radar
120.85	Ronaldsway Approach/Radar
120.90	Belfast (Aldergrove) Radar/Benson Approach
120.95	
121.00	Heathrow Tower
121.05	Leeds Radar
121.10	Dublin Approach
121.15	
121.20	Cardiff Tower/Edinburgh Approach
121.25	Aberdeen Radar/Manston Tower
121.30	Southampton Zone/Glasgow Radar

121.35	Manchester Radar
121.40	Leavesden Radar/Shannon Radar
121.45	
121.50	DISTRESS
121.55	
121.60	Fire and Rescue Services/Wycombe GMC
121.65	
> 121.70	Heathrow GMC/Manchester Tower/Aberdeen GMC/ Glasgow GMC
121.75	Luton Tower/Gatwick GMC/Edinburgh GMC
121.80	Birmingham GMC/Dublin GMC
121.85	Heathrow Departure Information/Aberdeen ATIS
> 121.90	Jersey GMC/Heathrow GMC/Castledon GMC
121.95	Halfpenny Green GMC/Gatwick GMC GMP/Oxford ATIS
122.00	Coventry Radar/Ford Tower/Lashenden Tower/Wattisham Tower/Baldonnel Approach
122.05	Company frequency (various)
122.10	Benson Tower/Brize Norton Radar/Church Fenton Tower/ Culdrose Tower/Finningley Tower/Leuchars Tower/Lyneham Radar/Shawbury Tower
122.15	Flotta/Leavesden Tower/Approach/Aberporth AFIS
122.20	Huddersfield (Crosland Moor)/Tatenhill/Cambridge Tower/ Haverfordwest
122.25	Leicester/Rochester/Caernarfon/Brent Oilfield, North Sea
122.30	Blackbushe/Bristol Filton Tower/Lands End St Just A/G/Perth (Scone) Approach/Sibson
122.35	Hethel/Audley End/Rush Green/Company frequency
122.375	Strubby Heliport (Lincs) Management Aviation
122.40	Little Snoring/Elstree/Dounreay Tower & Approach/Scatsta Radar
122.425	Earls Colne
122.45	Belfast (Harbour) Radar/Goodwood Approach/Sleap/Wickenby
122.50	Farnborough Tower/Weston Super Mare Tower
122.55	Dunsfold Approach/Mildenhall/West Freugh Tower
122.60	Inverness Tower/Plymouth (Roborough) Tower/Seething/ Sherburn-in-Elmet Tower/Swansea Tower/White Waltham
122.65	
122.70	Barton/Compton Abbas/Sywell/Silverstone/Bodmin/Tiree
122.75	
122.80	Nottingham/Stapleford Tawney/Heather Oilfield Scotland
122.85	Cranfield Approach/Eglinton Tower/Approach
> 122.90	Battersea Heliport/Dundee Tower/St Mawgan Tower/ Staverton Approach/Doncaster
122.95	Stourport Heliport/Ekofisk Oilfield North Sea

123.00	Halfpenny Green/Paull/Peterborough (Conington)
123.05	Bristol Filton Radar/Fenland/Peterhead Heliport (Brittair)/ Stevenage/Old Warden Shuttleworth Collection/West Sole and Viking Oilfields/Shipdham
123.10	Search and Rescue (Scene of Search) Frequency
123.15	Humberside Approach/Shoreham Tower/Sumburgh Approach/ Port Ellen
123.20	Cranfield Tower/Plymouth Approach/Barrow Tower
123.25	Isle of Wight (Bembridge)/Bridlington/Ipswich
123.30	Culdrose Radar/Finningley Radar/Leuchars Radar/ Lossiemouth Tower/Marham Radar/Machrihanish Radar/ Northolt Radar/St Mawgan Radar/Shawbury Radar/Topcliffe Tower/Valley Radar/Wattisham Radar
123.35	Hatfield Approach/Hawarden Approach
123.40	Lyneham Tower/Approach/Wattisham Radar/Wethersfield MATZ
123.45	Great Yarmouth (North Denes)/Redhill/Bristol Helicopters
123.425	Fairoaks
123.50	Dunkeswell/Duxford/Isle of Wight Sandown/Netherthorpe Newtownards/Shobdon/Stornoway/Strathallan
123.55	Various oil rigs in the North Sea
123.60	Cambridge Approach/Carlisle Tower & Approach/Alderney Tower
123.65	Gamston/Coal Aston (Sheffield)/Heathrow Executive Handling
123.70	Amsterdam Radar
123.75	Leeds Approach
123.80	Stansted Radar
123.85	
123.90	London ACC/Inbounds via Epsom/Ockham
123.95	Oceanic Clearance for Aircraft registered west of 30°W
124.00	Castledon Tower
124.05	
124.10	Paris Information (east sector)
124.15	Marham Radar/Portland Radar/Shawbury Approach/Ternhill
124.20	Manchester Zone
124.225	Gatwick Tower
124.25	Edinburgh Radar/Norwich Radar
124.30	Amsterdam FIS
124.325	Dunsfold Tower
124.35	Bristol (Lulsgate) Radar
124.40	Bedford Radar/Brawdy Radar/Topcliffe Radar
124.45	Scottish Control Low Level Far North/Warton Radar/ Samlesbury

124.50	Guernsey Radar
124.55	Copenhagen Control
124.60	London Flight Information (East of Amber One)
124.65	Dublin Control
124.70	Shannon Control
124.75	London Flight Information (West of Amber One)
124.80	Rome Airways
124.85	
124.90	Scottish Control/Manston Tower
124.95	Hawarden Tower/Bristol Filton Tower
125.00	Brussels Control South Sector
125.05	Southend Radar
125.10	Manchester Control Red 3 Amber 25 Low Level
125.15	Paris Radio (Met) (in French)
125.20	Jersey Zone
125.25	Farnborough Zone
125.30	Ronaldsway Radar
125.35	Boscombe Down Approach/Binbrook Radar/Middle Wallop MATZ
125.40	Shoreham Tower/Yeovil (Judwin) Tower
125.45	Paris Control
125.50	Moscow Control
125.55	St Mawgan Radar/Stansted Zone
125.60	Bournemouth (Hurn) Tower
125.65	Staverton Tower
125.70	Paris Information
125.75	Amsterdam Radar
125.80	London Control Radar Departures via Brookmans Park and Clacton
125.85	Cardiff Approach
125.875	Gatwick Radar
125.90	Coltishall Radar/Macrihanish Approach
125.95	London Control Inbounds via Lambourne
126.00	Paris Radio (Met) (in English)
126.05	Pailton Test (Near Rugby)
126.10	North Sea Radio/Highland Radar
126.15	Dusseldorf Control
126.20	Amsterdam Met
126.25	Scottish Control
126.30	London Control Inbounds via Bovingdon
126.35	Newcastle Approach/Manston Radar
126.40	Bordeaux Radio (Met) (in English)
126.45	London Control
	NORTHOLT TWR

126.50	Church Fenton Approach/Coningsby MATZ/Leuchars Approach/St Mawgan Approach
126.55	Wycombe Air Park (Booker)
126.60	London Volmet North
126.65	Manchester Control
126.70	Lydd Tower
126.75	Brussels (West Sector)
126.80	Copenhagen (North)
126.85	Scottish (South West)
126.90	Brussels Information
126.925	Woodford Tower
126.95	Stansted Approach
127.00	Dublin Volmet
127.05	Frankfurt Control
127.10	London Airways Lydd Sector West (Blue 3) and Cross Channel
127.15	
127.20	Zurich Volmet
127.25	Cotswold Radar
127.30	Luton Radar
127.35	Waddington Radar/Yeovilton Radar
127.40	Bremen Met
127.45	Milan Control
127.50	Shannon Control
127.55	Heathrow Radar
127.60	
127.65	Oceanic Clearance for Aircraft registered east of 30°W (Including Australia)
127.70	London Control Southern England and Cross Channel
127.75	Bristol Lulsgate Approach
127.80	Brussels Met
127.85	Reims Control
127.90	Shannon Control
127.95	London Control
128.00	Dublin Control
128.05	London Control North West, Red 3, Blue 1, High Level (Irish Sea)
128.10	Paris North East
128.15	Exeter Approach
128.175	Manchester ATIS
128.20	Brussels East
128.25	London Military
128.30	Aberdeen Radar/Netheravon A/G
128.35	Dutch Military

128.40	London Control—Radar departures via Detling and Hornchurch
128.45	Manston Approach
128.50	Scottish Control TMA
128.55	Upper Heyford
128.60	London Volmet South
128.65	Guernsey Approach
128.70	London Military Radar
128.75	Luton Approach
128.80	Brussels North
128.85	Southampton Tower/Approach/Teeside Director
128.90	London Control (TMA)
128.95	Southend Approach
129.00	Brest Control
129.05	Honington MATZ
129.10	Winthorpe (Glider Club)
129.15	Linton-on-Ouse MATZ
129.20	London Airways/Cardiff Sector
129.25	Warsaw ACC
129.30	Amsterdam ACC
129.35	Paris West
129.40	Biggin Hill Tower
129.45	Kent Radar
129.50	
129.55	Luton Approach
129.60	London Control South East England Red North and South Blue 29 (Clacton Sector)
129.65	Brussels Control East Sector
129.70	Company Frequency (World/Wardair/KLM) Fort William Heliport
129.75	BMA Ops/Air Europe Ops/UK Gatwick/Air Express/Bourn Air/BAC Filton Ops
129.80	Humberside Tower/Popham/Bourn
129.85	Hawarden Radar/West Malling
129.875	Enstone
129.90	South Marston/Hang Gliders/Hardwick (Norwich Mindacre Crop Sprayers) Langar Parachute Club
129.95	Cormorant Rigs, Scotland, North Sea
130.00	Bedford (Thurleigh)/Tower/Boscombe Down Tower
130.05	Farnborough Radar/Sumburgh Director/Woodford Approach/ West Freugh MATZ
130.10	Gliders
130.125	Gliders
130.15	Deptford Down (Salisbury Plain) Ops

130.20	Cottesmore Radar/Chivenor Radar
130.25	Abingdon Tower
130.275	Henstridge
130.30	Oxford Approach/Sturgate
130.35	Northolt Radar (On request)
130.40	Gliders
130.425	Halton
130.45	Thruxton/Skegness Common Frequency/Wellesbourne
130.475	Retford/Gamston
130.50	Moscow Control
130.55	Brough Tower/Andrews Field/Brands Hatch (Shawline Ops)
130.60	British Caledonian Ops/Pan Am Ops/Serviceair Ops
130.65	Dan-Air Ops (Manchester)
130.70	Bedford (Thurleigh) Approach
130.75	Belfast (Harbour) Tower/Boscombe Down Radar/Cambridge Radar/Woodford Radar
130.80	Hatfield Tower/Hucknall/Samlesbury Tower/Warton Tower/ Yeovil (Judwin) Approach
130.85	Belfast Harbour Approach/Bristol (Filton) Approach
130.90	Rome Radar
130.95	Marseille Control
131.00	Southampton Radar
131.05	London Control North East UIR (Pole Hill)
131.10	Brussels Control (West Sector)
131.15	Shannon Control (Cork Sector)
131.20	London Control West and Southern England Amber 25, White 39 Green 1 Red 14 (Strumble)
131.25	
131.30	Lydd (Ferryfield) Radar/Scottish ACC (Stornoway)
131.35	Paris Control North
131.40	Company Frequency Pan Am
131.45	Company Frequencies:- Air Canada/NLM/UK/Alitalia
131.425	131.475
131.50	Aer Lingus Ops (Dublin and Shannon)/KLM London
131.55	Company Frequency
131.60	TWA Ops/Air India Ops
131.65	KLM Schipol — 131.625
131.70	Swissair Ops
131.675	Britannia Ops
131.75	Aer Lingus Ops
131.775	Orion Ops
131.80	British Airways Speedbird Ops (Domestic) ← 131.875. Danair Ops Gatwick/ Quantas!
131.85	British Airways Speedbird Ops (Domestic)
131.90	British Airways Speedbird Ops (Overseas)

131.95	Iberia Airlines Ops/Sabena Ops
131.975	British Airways Ops (Glasgow)
132.00	Paris Control (Hand-overs from London 127.7 134.45)
132.05	London Control TMA (Outbounds)
132.10	Paris Control
132.15	Shannon Control
132.20	Euro Control (Maastricht Control Hand-overs from London 127.1)
132.25	Midland Radar (North Luffenham)
132.30	London Airways (Hurn Sector)
132.35	New Milligen (Dutch Military Radar)/Bristol (Filton) Radar
132.40	Leeming Radar
132.45	London Airways (Lydd East Sector)
132.50	Paris Control North
132.55	Madrid Control
132.60	London Control Southern England UIR. West of UA1 and South of UB1
132.65	
132.70	London Control Western England Amber 1 North of Dean Cross (Pole Hill) (THAMES/CITY)
132.75	
132.80	London Control (Bristol Sector)
132.85	
132.90	Border Radar (Boulmer)
132.95	Moscow Control
133.00	Brest Control
133.05	Manchester Control Airways Low Level Blue 1
133.075	Heathrow ATIS
133.10	Bordeaux Control
133.15	Cotswold Radar
133.20	Scottish FIS
133.25	Maastricht Control
133.30	London Military Radar
133.35	
133.40	Zurich Control
133.45	London Control Clacton
133.50	Paris Control North
133.55	Lee on Solent Approach
133.60	London Control High Level
133.65	Rhein Control
133.70	London Control Central England, Daventry Sector
133.75	Madrid Control
133.80	Oceanic Tracks Broadcast
133.85	Masstricht Control

133.90	London Military Radar
133.95	Maastricht Control
134.00	Scottish FIS
134.05	Wyton Radar/Culdrose
134.10	Highland Radar
134.15	Northolt Approach
134.20	
134.25	London Control North East Blue 1 East of Ottringham
134.30	Brize Radar/Eastern Radar (Watton)/Highland Radar
134.35	Valley Radar/Farnborough Radar
134.40	Reims Control
134.45	London Control (Hurn Sector)
134.50	
134.55	Chelmsford Heliport/Rivenhall Heliport
134.60	Zurich Control
134.65	
134.70	London FIS North of Blue 1
134.75	London Control (Daventry Sector)
134.80	Rhein Control
134.85	Border Radar RAF Boulmer
134.90	London Control (Dover Sector)
134.95	Rhein Control
135.00	
135.05	London Control (Seaford Sector)
135.10	
135.15	London Military Radar
135.20	Eastern Radar (Military)
135.25	London Control Central and Southern England, Amber 2 (Daventry Sector)
135.30	Paris Control North
135.35	Dusseldorf Information
135.40	
135.45	Maastricht Control
135.50	Reims Control
135.55	
135.60	Shannon Control (Shannon Sector)
135.65	Brest Control
135.70	Lee on Solent Tower
135.75	
135.80	Paris Control
135.85	Scottish Control
135.90	Paris Control
135.95	Blackpool Approach

Appendix 4

UHF air band frequencies

Some of the more advanced radio receivers are capable of monitoring the UHF frequencies used by military aircraft and the RAF and USAF bases in the UK. In response to demand this listing has been compiled from sources available to the general public.

Frequencies of airports and airfields

Aberporth: AFIS: 375.9
Abingdon: Tower: 246.4 Radar: 260.1/227.0/344.0
Alconbury: Tower: 248.35/257.8 GMC: 365.65 Approach (Wyton): 338.1/362.3/255.7 OPS: 377.8/382.5
Barkston Heath: Tower: 281.6 Approach 228.6
Bedford: Tower: 262.6 Approach: 356.0/377.15 PAR: 255.8
Benson: Tower: 337.8 Approach: 347.1/362.3 Radar: 254.4/ 227.0/344.0
Bentwaters: Tower: 257.8/395.2 GMC: 341.4 Approach: 263.4 PAR: 252.2/386.0 OPS: 246.0/347.45
Binbrook: Tower: 387.7/257.8 Approach/Radar: 357.0/362.3/254.3/229.2/344.0 PAR: 285.9/394.0
Bishops Court: A/G: 345.5
Border Radar: 228.5
Boscombe Down: Tower: 242.2 Approach/Radar: 228.2/289.8 PAR: 279.8 Zone: 399.3 ATIS: 378.8
Boulmer: A/G: 226.5/282.8
Brawdy: Tower: 315.4/257.8 GMC: 250.7 Approach: 276.2/362.3/313.2/338.3 PAR: 257.7/376.0
Bristol/Filton: Tower: 395.2 Approach/Radar: 346.25/352.8
Brize Norton: Tower: 275.6/257.8 GMC: 281.4 Approach/Radar: 341.3/292.4/387.5 PAR: 251.0/385.4 OPS: 360.4 ATIS: 396.7
Brough: Approach/Radar: 277.1
Cambridge: Tower/Radar: 294.6
Cardiff: Approach: 252.2
Chivenor: Tower: 345.5 GMC: 387.65 Approach/Radar: 309.7/362.3/395.6/354.7/228.0 ZONE: 343.2

Church Fenton: Tower: 308.9/257.8 Approach/Radar: 374.0/362.3/306.8/388.2/290.4/286.0/344.0
Coltishall: Tower: 361.0 Approach/Radar: 232.4/394.05/286.35 PAR: 368.35/246.65
Coningsby: Tower: 227.7 GMC: 345.85 Approach/Radar: 229.5/342.2/344.0/362.3 PAR: 311.6/232.0
Cosford: Tower: 345.3 Approach: 335.7/362.3
Cottesmore: Tower: 275.5/257.8 GMC: 228.85 Approach/Radar: 379.4/394.5/367.2/236.5 PAR: 386.8/354.65
Cranfield: Tower: 294.6 Approach/Radar: 315.5
Cranwell: Tower: 292.7/257.8 GMC: 337.0 Approach/Radar: 278.7/362.3/253.3/241.8/344.0 PAR: 364.8/358.2
Croughton: A/G 343.6
Culdrose: Tower: 277.2 GMC: 362.3 Approach/Radar: 326.0/286.7 PAR: 279.0/226.2
Dishforth: Tower: 337.4 Approach: 368.8
Dunsfold: Tower: 289.6 Approach/Radar: 277.6/394.7
Eastern Radar: 354.7
Edinburgh: Approach/Radar 362.3
Elvington: Tower: 258.5 Approach: 345.7
Fairford: Tower: 387.6 Approach/Radar: 318.1/314.4 PAR: 375.9 OPS: 276.05
Finningley: Tower: 336.7 GMC: 230.0 Approach/Radar: 396.8/226.6/267.2/344.0 PAR: 381.5/385.4
Glasgow: Approach/Radar: 362.3
Greenham Common: Tower: 275.75 GMC: 246.55
Hatfield: Tower: 363.5 Approach/Radar: 369.3
Hawarden: Tower: 226.4
Highland Radar: 355.2/337.4
Honington: Tower: 399.7/257.8 GMC: 387.65 Approach/Radar: 373.2/362.3/286.4/376.8/226.35/344.0 PAR: 297.9/385.4
Inverness: Approach: 362.3
Kemble: Tower: 341.7 Approach/Radar: 300.4/362.3/381.8/264.2
Kinloss: Tower: 354.7/257.8 Approach/Radar: 394.1/226.2/344.0 PAR: 227.2/230.0 OPS: 289.1
Lakenheath: Tower: 360.9/257.8 GMC: 315.7 Approach/Radar: 286.4/376.8/316.5/343.9/263.35/366.75/385.4/344.0/277.2 OPS: 315.7/253.55
Leconfield: A/G: 297.8/282.8
Leeming: Radar: 359.2/362.3
Lee-on-Solent: Tower: 376.5
Leuchars: Tower: 245.6 GMC: 280.2 Approach/Radar: 289.7/362.3/276.2 PAR: 318.9/353.85 OPS: 343.0
Linton-on-Ouse: Tower: 376.5/257.8 GMC: 346.7 Approach/Radar: 276.0/290.4/344.0/388.2 PAR: 387.6/250.7
Llanbedr: Tower: 294.6 Approach/Radar: 365.9 PAR: 387.25

London Military: Initial Contact Frequency: North: 342.8 South: 265.7 Pole Hill/Irish Sea: 225.8 Daventry: 353.2 Clacton: 290.2 Dover/Lydd: 354.0 Seaford/Hurn: 250.6

Lossiemouth: Tower: 291.7 GMC: 354.0 Approach/Radar: 394.1/362.3/318.5/344.0 PAR: 279.0/229.3

Luton: Radar: 398.0

Lyneham: Tower: 346.5 GMC: 386.1 Approach/Radar: 339.1/362.3/287.9/362.5/344.0 PAR: 248.4/385.4 OPS: 354.45 ATIS: 276.3

Macrihanish: Tower: 352.65/257.8 Approach/Radar: 229.95/362.3/318.55/344.0 PAR: 387.6/385.4

Manston: Tower: 294.1/257.8 Approach/Radar: 287.4/362.3/387.0/344.0 PAR: 345.5/385.4

Marham: Tower: 336.0/257.8 Approach/Radar: 346.2/362.3/318.7/344.0 PAR: 369.5/385.4 OPS: 290.95

Merryfield: Tower: 259.0

Middle Wallop: Tower: 364.0/257.8 Approach: 338.8 Radar: 229.1/286.0

Midland Radar: 244.3

Mildenhall: Tower: 243.3 GMC: 282.7 Approach (Honington): 373.2/376.8 OPS: 277.3/335.5

Netheravon: Tower: 229.0 Approach: 229.7

Newcastle: Approach/Radar: 226.1

Newton: Tower: 360.3/257.8 Approach: 227.5/362.3

Northolt: Tower: 233.1/257.8 Approach/Radar: 309.2/362.3/355.4 PAR: 234.9 OPS: 368.3 ATIS: 259.2

Odiham: Tower: 255.75/257.8 Approach/Radar: 377.4/362.3/394.6 PAR: 356.95/385.4 ATIS: 241.4

Portland: Tower: 291.7/362.3 A/G: 282.8 Approach/Radar: 328.5 PAR: 394.1

Predannack: Tower: 354.4 Approach (Culdrose) 326.0

Prestwick: Tower/Approach: 257.8/231.9 OPS: 291.7

St Athan: Tower: 336.0/257.8 Approach/Radar: 252.2/311.4/362.3/354.2/344.0 PAR: 395.5/385.4

St Mawgan: Tower: 288.1 Approach/Radar: 354.8/362.3/226.6/344.0 PAR: 387.6 OPS: 254.2

Salisbury Plain: A/G: 338.6

Samlesbury: Tower: 231.7 Approach (Warton): 352.8

Scampton: Tower: 227.1/257.8 GMC: 269.4 Approach/Radar: 251.6/228.3/362.3/301.6/344.0 PAR: 376.1/314.3

Scottish Military 287.0

Sculthorpe: Tower: 276.35/257.8 GMC: 251.5 Approach/Radar: 355.9/143.3 PAR: 261.35/310.45/378.3/275.65/148.25

Shawbury: Tower: 226.7/257.8 GMC: 228.4 Approach/Radar: 346.0/362.3/347.5/265.2/344.0 PAR: 341.5/385.4

Shetland Radar: 227.3

Stornoway: Tower/Approach: 340.3

Swinderby: Tower: 275.7 Approach: 394.3

Teeside: Tower: 395.5 Approach/Radar: 397.5

Ternhill: Tower: 287.4 Approach/Radar: 229.6/362.3/228.1

Topcliffe: Tower: 377.1/257.8 Approach/Radar: 387.2/362.3/345.1/385.4

Upavon: Tower: 374.9 OPS: 398.95

Upper Heyford: Tower: 386.15/257.8 GMC: 370.9 Approach/Radar: 346.1/362.3 PAR: 341.9/312.6/307.05/231.45 OPS: 369.7/310.35 ATIS: 382.35

Valley: Tower: 381.1/257.8 GMC: 230.0 Approach/Radar: 337.3/362.3/394.9/253.1/344.0 PAR: 369.5/385.4 SAR: 282.8

Waddington: Tower: 315.4/257.8 Approach/Radar: 245.5/362.3/344.0/354.8 PAR: 319.0/385.4

Warton: Tower: 231.7 Approach/Radar: 352.8/231.7/369.3

Wattisham: Tower: 399.0 Approach/Radar: 234.7/362.3/290.5/344.0 PAR: 319.2/310.5

West Freugh: Tower: 262.6 Approach/Radar: 395.95/375.9

Wethersfield: Tower: 241.35/257.8 GMC: 252.7 Approach/Radar: 362.3/396.6/344.15/383.2/268.25/296.6/342.0 OPS: 343.9

Wittering: Tower: 241.9/257.8/142.29 GMC: 281.95 Approach/Radar: 354.9/362.3/236.5/344.0 PAR: 311.95/269.6

Woodbridge: Tower: 257.8/398.1 GMC: 241.5 Approach/Radar (Bentwaters): 263.4/386.0 OPS: 246.0/347.45

Woodford: Tower/Approach: 366.6/243.4

Woodvale: Tower: 229.5 Approach: 345.6

Wyton: Tower: 339.1/257.8 Approach/Radar: 338.1/362.3/225.7/225.6/344.0 PAR: 376.0/385.4 OPS: 395.7

Yeovil: Tower: 294.6 Approach: 364.3 Radar: 226.0/236.4

Yeovilton: Tower: 310.2/291.7 GMC: 362.3 Approach/Radar: 293.8/353.0 PAR: 249.4/296.3 ATIS: 347.4

Airband frequencies in numerical order

MHz	
142.29	Wittering Tower
143.30	Sculthorpe Approach/Radar
148.25	Sculthorpe PAR
225.60	Wyton Approach/Radar
225.80	London Military Initial Contact Frequency Pole Hill/Irish Sea
226.00	Yeovil Radar
226.10	Newcastle Approach/Radar
226.20	Kinloss Approach/Radar
226.35	Honington Approach/Radar
226.40	Hawarden Tower
226.50	Boulmer A/G
226.60	St. Mawgan Approach/Radar

226.70	Shawbury Tower
227.00	Abingdon Radar/Benson Radar
227.10	Scampton Tower
227.20	Kinloss PAR
227.30	Shetland Radar
227.50	Newton Approach
227.70	Coningsby Tower
228.00	Chivenor Approach/Radar
228.10	Ternhill Approach/Radar
228.20	Boscombe Down Approach/Radar
228.30	Scampton Approach/Radar
228.40	Shawbury GMC
228.50	Border Radar
228.60	Barkston Heath Approach
228.85	Cottesmore GMC
229.00	Netheravon Tower
229.10	Middle Wallop Radar
229.20	Binbrook Approach/Radar
229.30	Lossiemouth PAR
229.40	Woodvale Tower
229.50	Coningsby Approach/Radar
229.60	Ternhill Approach/Radar
229.70	Netheravon Approach
229.95	Macrihanish Approach/Radar
230.00	Finningley GMC/Kinloss PAR/Valley GMC
231.45	Upper Heyford PAR
231.70	Samlesbury Tower/Warton Tower/Approach/Radar
231.90	Prestwick Tower/Approach
232.00	Coningsby PAR
232.40	Coltishall Approach/Radar
233.10	Northolt Tower
234.70	Wattisham Approach/Radar
234.90	Northolt PAR
236.40	Yeovil Radar
236.50	Cottesmore Approach/Radar: Wittering Approach/Radar
241.35	Wethersfield Tower
241.40	Odiham ATIS
241.50	Woodbridge GMC
241.80	Cranwell Approach/Radar

241.90	Wittering Tower
242.20	Boscombe Down Tower
243.30	Mildenhall Tower
243.40	Woodford Tower/Approach
244.30	Midland Radar
245.50	Waddington Approach/Radar
245.60	Leuchars Tower
246.00	Bentwaters OPS/Woodbridge OPS
246.40	Abingdon Tower
246.55	Greenham Common Tower
246.65	Coltishall PAR
248.35	Alconbury Tower
248.40	Lyneham PAR
249.40	Yeovilton PAR
250.60	London Military Initial Contact Frequency Seaford/Hurn
250.70	Brawdy GMC/Linton-on-Ouse PAR
251.00	Brize Norton PAR
251.50	Sculthorpe GMC
251.60	Scampton Approach/Radar
252.20	Bentwaters PAR/Cardiff Approach/St. Athan Approach/Radar
252.70	Wethersfield GMC
253.10	Valley Approach/Radar
253.30	Cranwell Approach/Radar
253.55	Lakenheath OPS
254.20	St. Athan Approach/Radar/St. Mawgan OPS
254.30	Binbrook Approach/Radar
254.40	Benson Radar
255.70	Alconbury Approach (Wyton): Wyton Approach/Radar
255.75	Odiham Tower
255.80	Bedford PAR
257.70	Brawdy PAR
257.80	Common Tower Frequency: Alconbury/Bentwaters/Binbrook/Brawdy/Brize Norton/Church Fenton/Cottesmore/Cranwell/Honington/Kinloss/Lakenheath/Linton-on-Ouse/Macrihanish/Manston/Marham/Middle Wallop/Newton/Northolt/Odiham/Prestwick/St. Athan/Scampton/Sculthorpe/Shawbury/Topcliffe/Upper Heyford/Valley/Waddington/Wethersfield/Wittering/Woodbridge/Wyton

258.50	Elvington Tower
259.00	Merryfield Tower
259.20	Northolt ATIS
260.10	Abingdon Radar
261.35	Sculthorpe PAR
262.60	Bedford Tower/West Freugh Tower
263.35	Lakenheath Approach/Radar
263.40	Bentwaters Approach: Woodbridge Approach/Radar (Bentwaters)
264.20	Kemble Approach/Radar
265.20	Shawbury Approach/Radar
265.70	London Military Initial Contact Frequency South
267.20	Finningley Approach/Radar
268.25	Wethersfield Approach/Radar
269.40	Scampton GMC
269.60	Wittering PAR
275.50	Cottesmore Tower
275.60	Brize Norton Tower
275.65	Sculthorpe PAR
275.70	Swinderby Tower
275.75	Greenham Common Tower
276.00	Linton-on-Ouse Approach/Radar
276.05	Fairford OPS
276.20	Brawdy Approach/Leuchars Approach/Radar
276.30	Lyneham ATIS
276.35	Sculthorpe Tower
277.10	Brough Radar Approach
277.20	Culdrose Tower/Lakenheath Approach/Radar
277.30	Mildenhall OPS
277.60	Dunsfold Approach/Radar
278.70	Cranwell Approach/Radar
279.00	Culdrose PAR/Lossiemouth PAR
279.80	Boscombe Down PAR
280.20	Leuchars GMC
281.40	Brize Norton GMC
281.60	Barkston Heath Tower

281.95	Wittering Tower
282.70	Mildenhall GMC
282.80	Boulmer A/G: Leconfield A/G: Portland A/G: Valley SAR
285.90	Binbrook PAR
286.00	Church Fenton Approach/Fenton: Middle Wallop Radar
286.35	Coltishall Approach/Radar
286.40	Honington Approach/Radar: Lakenheath Approach/Radar
286.70	Culdrose Approach/Radar
287.00	Scottish Military
287.40	Manston Approach/Radar: Ternhill Tower
287.90	Lyneham Approach/Tower
288.10	St. Mawgan Tower
289.10	Kinloss OPS
289.60	Dunsfold Tower
289.70	Leuchars Approach/Radar
289.80	Boscombe Down Approach/Radar
290.05	Marham OPS
290.20	London Military Initial Contact Frequency Clacton
290.40	Church Fenton Approach/Radar: Linton-on-Ouse Approach/ Radar
290.50	Wattisham Approach/Radar
291.70	Lossiemouth Tower: Portland Tower: Prestwick OPS: Yeovilton Tower
292.40	Brize Norton Approach/Radar
292.70	Cranwell Tower
293.80	Yeovilton Approach/Radar
294.10	Manston Tower
294.60	Cambridge Tower/Radar: Cranfield Tower: Llanbedr Tower: Yeovil Tower
296.30	Yeovilton PAR
296.60	Wethersfield Approach/Radar
297.80	Leconfield A/G
297.90	Honigton PAR
300.40	Kemble Approach/Radar
301.60	Scampton Approach/Radar
306.80	Church Fenton Approach/Radar

307.05	Upper Heyford PAR
308.90	Church Fenton Tower
309.20	Northolt Approach/Radar
309.70	Chivenor Approach/Radar
310.20	Yeovilton Tower
310.35	Upper Heyford OPS
310.45	Sculthorpe PAR
310.50	Wattisham PAR
311.40	St. Athan Approach/Radar
311.60	Coningsby PAR
311.95	Wittering PAR
312.60	Upper Heyford PAR
313.20	Brawdy Approach
314.30	Scampton PAR
314.40	Fairford Approach/Radar
315.40	Brawdy Tower: Waddington Tower
315.50	Cranfield Approach/Radar
315.70	Lakenheath GMC/Lakenheath OPS
316.50	Lakenheath Approach/Radar
318.10	Fairford Approach/Radar
318.50	Lossiemouth Approach/Radar
318.55	Macrihanish Approach/Radar
318.70	Marham Approach/Radar
318.90	Leuchars PAR
319.00	Waddington PAR
319.20	Wattisham PAR
326.00	Culdrose Approach/Radar: Predannack Approach (Culdrose)
328.50	Portland Approach/Radar
335.50	Mildenhall OPS
335.70	Cosford Approach
336.00	Marham Tower: St. Athan Tower
336.60	Woodford Tower/Approach
336.70	Finningley Tower
337.00	Cranwell GMC
337.30	Valley Approach/Radar
337.40	Dishforth Tower/Highland Radar

337.80	Benson Tower
338.10	Alconbury Approach (Wyton)/Wyton Approach/Radar
338.30	Brawdy Approach
338.60	Salisbury Plain A/G
338.80	Middle Wallop Approach
339.10	Lyneham Approach/Radar
340.30	Stornoway Tower/Approach
341.30	Brize Norton Approach/Radar
341.40	Bentwaters GMC
341.50	Shawbury PAR
341.70	Kemble Tower
341.90	Upper Heyford Par
342.00	Wethersfield Approach/Radar
342.20	Coningsby Approach/Radar
342.80	London Military Initial Contact Frequency North
343.00	Leuchars OPS
343.20	Chivenor Zone
343.60	Croughton A/G
343.90	Lakenheath Approach/Radar: Wethersfield OPS
344.00	Common Approach/Radar Frequency: Abingdon/Benson/Binbrook/Church Fenton/Coningsby/Cranwell/Finningley/Honington/Kinloss/Lakenheath/Linton-on-Ouse/Lossiemouth/Lyneham/Macrihanish/Manston/Marham/St. Athan/St. Mawgan/Scampton/Shawbury/Valley/Waddington/Wattisham/Wittering/Wyton
344.15	Wethersfield Approach/Radar
345.10	Topcliffe Approach/Radar
345.30	Cosford Tower
345.50	Bishops Court A/G: Chivenor Tower: Manston PAR
345.60	Woodvale Approach
345.70	Elvington Approach
345.85	Coningsby GMC
346.00	Shawbury Approach/Radar
346.10	Upper Heyford Approach/Radar
346.20	Marham Approach/Radar
346.25	Bristol/Filton Approach/Radar
346.50	Lyneham Tower
346.70	Linton-on-Ouse GMC
347.10	Benson Approach
347.40	Yeovilton ATIS

347.45	Bentwaters OPS: Woodbridge OPS
347.50	Shawbury Approach/Radar
352.65	Macrihanish Tower
352.80	Bristol/Filton Approach/Radar: Samlesbury Approach (Warton): Warton Approach/Radar
353.00	Yeovilton Approach/Radar
353.20	London Military Initial Contact Frequency Daventry
353.85	Leuchars PAR
354.00	London Military Initial Contact Frequency Dover/Lydd: Lossiemouth GMC
354.40	Predannack Tower
354.45	Lyneham OPS
354.65	Cottesmore PAR
354.70	Chivenor Approach/Radar: Eastern Radar (Watton): Kinloss Tower
354.80	St. Mawgan Approach/Radar: Waddington Approach/Radar
354.90	Wittering Approach/Radar
355.20	Highland Radar
355.40	Northolt Approach/Radar
355.90	Sculthorpe Approach/Radar
356.00	Bedford Approach
356.95	Odiham PAR
357.00	Binbrook Approach/Radar
358.20	Cranwell PAR
359.20	Leeming Radar
360.30	Newton Tower
360.40	Brize Norton OPS
360.90	Lakenheath Tower
361.00	Coltishall Tower
362.30	Cosford Approach: Culdrose GMC: Portland Tower: Yeovilton GMC Also Common Approach/Radar Frequency: Alconbury/Benson/Binbrook/Brawdy/Chivenor/Church Fenton/Coningsby/Cranwell/Edinburgh/Glasgow/Honington/Inverness/Kemble/Leeming/Leuchars/Lossiemouth/Lyneham/Macrihanish/Manston/Marham/Newton/Northolt/Odiham/St. Athan/St. Mawgan/Scampton/Shawbury/Ternhill/Topcliffe/Upper Heyford/Valley/Waddington/Wattisham/Wethersfield/Wyton

362.50	Lyneham Approach/Radar
364.00	Middle Wallop Tower
364.30	Yeovil Approach
364.80	Cranwell PAR
365.65	Alconbury GMC
365.90	Llanbedr Approach/Radar
366.75	Lakenheath Approach/Radar
367.20	Cottesmore Approach/Radar
368.30	Northolt OPS
368.35	Coltishall PAR
368.80	Dishforth Approach
369.30	Hatfield Approach/Radar: Warton Approach/Radar
369.50	Marham PAR: Valley PAR
369.70	Upper Heyford OPS
370.90	Upper Heyford GMC
373.20	Honington Approach/Radar: Mildenhall Approach (Honington)
374.00	Church Fenton Approach/Radar
374.90	Upavon Tower
375.90	Aberporth AFIS: Fairford PAR: West Freugh Approach/Radar
376.00	Brawdy PAR: Wyton PAR
376.10	Scampton PAR
376.50	Lee-on-Solent Tower/Linton-on-Ouse Tower
376.80	Honington Approach/Radar: Lakenheath Approach/Radar: Mildenhall Approach (Honington)
377.10	Topcliffe Tower
377.15	Bedford Approach
377.40	Odiham Approach/Radar
377.80	Alconbury Dispatcher
378.30	Sculthorpe PAR
378.80	Boscombe Down ATIS
379.40	Cottesmore Approach/Radar
381.10	Valley Tower
381.50	Finningley PAR
381.80	Kemble Approach/Radar
382.35	Upper Heyford ATIS
382.50	Alconbury Command Post

383.20	Wethersfield Approach/Radar
385.40	Common PAR Frequency: Brize Norton/Finningley/Honington/Lakenheath/Lyneham/ Macrihanish/Manston/Marham/Odiham/St. Athan/Shawbury/ Topcliffe/Valley/Waddington/Wyton
386.00	Bentwaters Dep Con/Woodbridge Approach/Radar (Bentwaters)
386.10	Lyneham GMC
386.15	Upper Heyford Tower
386.80	Cottesmore PAR
387.00	Manston Approach/Radar
387.20	Topcliffe Approach/Radar
387.25	Llanbedr PAR
387.50	Brize Norton Approach/Radar
387.60	Fairford Tower/Linton-on-Ouse PAR/Macrihanish PAR/St. Mawgan PAR
387.65	Chivenor GMC/Honington GMC
387.70	Binbrook Tower
388.20	Church Fenton Approach/Radar: Linton-on-Ouse Approach/ Radar
394.00	Binbrook PAR
394.05	Coltishall Approach/Radar
394.10	Kinloss Approach/Radar: Lossiemouth Approach/Radar: Portland PAR
394.30	Swinderby Approach
394.50	Cottesmore Approach/Radar
394.60	Odiham Approach/Radar
394.70	Dunsfold Approach/Radar
394.90	Valley Approach/Radar
395.20	Bentwaters Tower: Bristol/Filton Tower
395.50	St. Athan PAR: Tees-side Tower
395.60	Chivenor Approach/Radar
395.70	Wyton OPS
395.95	West Freugh Approach/Radar
396.60	Wethersfield Approach/Radar
396.70	Brize Norton ATIS
396.80	Finningsley Approach/Radar
397.50	Tees-side Approach/Radar
398.00	Luton Radar
398.10	Woodbridge Tower

398.95	Upavon OPS
399.00	Wattisham Tower
399.10	Wyton Tower
399.30	Boscombe Down Zone
399.70	Honington Tower

Appendix 5

ICAO Aircraft type designators

The designators listed below are used for flight planning purposes and also by ATC on flight progress strips. The aircraft name or designation in full is normally used on the R/T but many of the abbreviated versions may also be heard. This list is a sample of the most common ones.

AA5	Grumman AA5
AC12	Rockwell 112
AC14	Rockwell 114
AC6T	Turbo Commander
AP2S	Super Guppy
B707	Boeing 707
B727	Boeing 727
B737	Boeing 737
B747	Boeing 747
B757	Boeing 757
B767	Boeing 767
BA11	BAe 111
BA46	BAe 146
BE10	Beech King Air 100
BE20	Super King Air 200
BE55	Beech Baron
BE60	Beech Duke
BE90	Beech King Air 90
BE95	Beech Travelair
BH06	Bell Jet Ranger
BN2	BN-2 Islander
BN3	BN-3 Trislander
BR31	Britannia
BT12	Pup
BT20	Basset/Beagle 206
C150	Cessna 150
C172	Cessna 172
C310	Cessna 310
C401	Cessna 401
C421	Cessna 421
C500	Cessna Citation
C550	Citation II
CV58	Convair 580
DA20	Falcon 20
DA50	Falcon 50
DH2	DHC-2 Beaver
DH6	DHC-6 Twin Otter
DH7	DHC-7 Dash 7
E110	Bandeirante
E121	Xingu
EA30	Airbus A300
FK27	Friendship
FK28	Fellowship
G2	Gulfstream II
G159	Gulfstream I
HP7	Herald
HS04	Dove
HS14	Heron
HS25	BAe 125
HS65	Argosy
HS74	BAe 748
HS82	BAe Hawk
IL18	Ilyushin IL-18
IL62	Ilyushin IL-62

L188	Lockheed Electra
LR24	Learjet 24
LR35	Learjet 35
ND16	C160 Transall
ND26	Nord 262
PA28	Cherokee
PA31	Navajo
PAZT	Aztec
PN68	Partenavia P68
S210	Caravelle
S601	Corvette
S880	Rallye
SC3	Bulldog
SC4	Jetstream
SF34	SAAB-Fairchild SF340
SH33	Shorts SD3-30
SH36	Shorts SD3-60
SW2	Merlin IIA
SW3	Merlin III
SW4	Merlin IV/Metro
TB09	TB-09 Tampico
TB10	TB-10 Tobago
TU34	Tupolev TU-134
TU54	Tupolev TU-154
VC7	Viscount 700
VC8	Viscount 800
VC9	Vanguard/Merchantman

Appendix 6

Aircraft radio callsigns

The callsign prefixes below include many officially allocated to various British operators, although in practice some are rarely used. A few military call signs to be heard over Britain have been incorporated as they have remained unchanged for many years.

Due to the limited number of combinations available in two-letter designators, it has been agreed by participating states of ICAO to convert to a three-letter system. The projected date for full conversion is 25 October 1987 but some operators are already using their allocations.

R/T callsign	2-letter code	3-letter code	Operation
Aerocharter	—	ACC	Aero Charter Midlands Ltd
Aeroflot	SU	AFL	Aeroflot
Aeronaut	—	CFD	Cranfield Institute of Technology
Aeropool	—	TPL	Turbopool
Aerostar	—	—	Mann Aviation Ltd
Aerotime	—	AET	Aerotime Ltd
Air Belgium	VY	ABB	Air Belgium
Air Berlin	AB	BER	Air Berlin
Airbridge	AK	ABR	Air Bridge Carriers Ltd
Air Canada	AC	ACA	Air Canada
Aircargo	—	FFL	Intavia Ltd
Aircontinental	CW	CWA	Air Continental Ltd
Air Coventry	—	COV	Air Coventry
Air Ecosse	WG	ECS	Air Ecosse Ltd
Air Europe	AE	AEL	Air Europe Ltd
Airevac	—	—	USAF ambulance flights
Air Ferry	VF	BAF	British Air Ferries
Air Force One	—	—	US Presidential aircraft
Air Force Two	—	—	Back-up Presidential aircraft with VIPs on board

R/T callsign	2-letter code	3-letter code	Operation
Airgo	—	—	Airgo Ltd
Air India	AI	AIC	Air India
Air London	GG	ACG	Air London
Airmove	—	—	Skywork Ltd
Air Nav	—	AAT	Air Navigation and Trading Co Ltd
Airwork	—	AWK	Airwork Services Training
Albion	—	ALA	Albion Aviation
Alitalia	AZ	AZA	Alitalia
All Charter	—	BLA	All Charter Ltd
Alton	—	—	Alton Towers Ltd
Aly Aviation	—	AAV	Aly Aviation
American	AA	AAL	American Airlines
Anglian	—	MHA	Anglian Air Taxis
Anglo	ML	ANC	Anglo Cargo Ltd
Aravco	—	ARV	Aravco
Armyair	—	AAC	Army Air Corps
Ascot	RR	RRR	RAF 1 Group (Air Transport)
Atlantic	DG	AAG	Atlantic Air Services
Austrian	OS	AUA	Austrian Airlines
Avro	—	WFD	Woodford BAe
AVT	—	AVT	ATS Aircharter Ltd
Ayline	GR	AUR	Aurigny Air Services Ltd
Backer	—	BCR	British Charter
BAFJET	—	—	British Air Ferries Business Jets Ltd
Balair	BB	BBB	Balair
Balkan	LZ	LAZ	Balkan-Bulgarian Airlines
Batman	WK	—	Ratioflug Frankfurt
Beatours	KT	BKT	British Airtours Ltd
Beaupair	—	AVB	Aviation Beauport Ltd
Beeline	—	BHE	Biggin Hill Executive Aviation Ltd
Birmex	—	BEX	Birmingham Executive Airways PLC
Bizair	—	—	Business Aircraft Users Association Ltd
Biztravel	—	BAT	Business Air Travel
Blackbox	—	RRS	Bedford RAE (RRS)
Blackburn	—	BBN	Scampton BAe
Bristol	—	FIL	Bristol BAe
Bristow	UH	BHL	Bristow Helicopters Group Ltd
Britannia	BY	BAL	Britannia Airways Ltd
British Island	KD	BIS	British Island Airways Ltd
Bryanair	—	BRN	Bryan Aviation
Brymon	PM	BRY	Brymon Airways
Busy Bee	BS	BEE	Busy Bee of Norway
Cabair	—	CBR	Cabair Air Taxis Ltd

R/T callsign	2-letter code	3-letter code	Operation
Caledonian	BR	BCA	British Caledonian Airways Ltd
Cambrian	—	LAW	Cardiff Aviation Ltd
Camelot	—	CME	Air Camelot
Carbon	—	SME	S M Exports Ltd
Casair	KS	CSL	Casair Aviation Services Ltd
Catbird	—	—	US Navy, Naples
Cathay	CX	CPX	Cathay Pacific Airways Ltd
Cayman	KX	CAY	Cayman Airways Ltd
Cedarjet			Middle East Airlines
Ceebee	—	CBH	CB Executive Helicopters
Cega	CN	CEG	Cega Aviation Ltd
Cessnair	—	—	Westair Flying Services Ltd
Chad	—	—	Chad Air Services Ltd
Chartair	—	—	Chartair Ltd
Cheyne	—	—	Cheyne Motors Ltd
City	—	NLM	City Hopper
Clipper	PA	PAA	Pan-American
Clog	—	—	Scholl (UK) Ltd
Clyde	—	CLY	Clyde Surveys Ltd
Colt	—	CEA	Colt Car Co
Condor	DF	CFG	Condor Flugdienst
Connectair	—	CAX	Connectair Ltd
County	—	CAK	County Air Services
Cyprus	CY	CYP	Cyprus
Danair	DA	DAN	Danair Services Ltd
Delta	DL	DAL	Delta Airlines
Deltair	DE	DAT	Delta Air Transport
Dodo	—	ASS	Air Sarnia
Dollar	—	DAS	Dollar Air Services
Donex	—	DNX	Donoghue Aviation
Dragon	—	WSH	Welsh Airways
Dravidian	—	DRA	Dravidian Air Services Ltd
Duke	—	—	207th Aviation Company, US Army, Heidelberg
Dynasty	—	—	China Airlines
Eagle	—	EAG	Eagle Air Ltd
Eastex	—	EAX	Eastern-Air Executive Ltd
Ecosse Air	WG	ECS	Air Ecosse Ltd
Egyptair	MS	MSR	Egyptair
El Al	LY	ELY	El Al
Elmair	—	ELM	Elmdon Aviation Ltd
EMA	—	EMA	East Midland Aviation Ltd
Empress	CP	—	CP-Air

R/T callsign	2-letter code	3-letter code	Operation
Euroair	EZ	URO	Euroair Transport Ltd
European	BC	BCS	European Air Transport
Evergreen	—		RAE
Exflight	—	EXF	Expressflight Ltd
Express	—	FDE	Federal Express
Expressair	LS	EXS	Express Air Services (CI) Ltd
Fairflight	FC	FGT	Fairflight Ltd
Falcon Jet	FN	FJC	Falcon Jet Centre
Fanum	—	—	Automobile Association
Fieldair	FS	FAS	Field Aircraft Services Ltd
Finnair	AY	FIN	Finnair
Flamingo	NS	NFD	Nurnburger Flugdienst
Flint	—	FSB	Flight Services International Ltd
Foxtrot Mike	—	—	French Air Force
Fordair	FD	FOB	Ford Motor Co Ltd
Foyle	UP	UPA	Air Foyle Ltd
Fox Club	—	—	Leicester Aero Club
Gama	—	GMX	Gama Aviation Ltd
Gatwick Air	—	WSC	Gatwick Air Taxis Ltd
Gauntlet	—	BDN	Boscombe Down MOD/PE
Gibair	GT	GBL	GB Airways Ltd
Gillair		GIL	Gill Aviation Ltd
Glen	—	GLH	Gleneagle Helicopters Services (Scotland) Ltd
Grosvenor	—	GRV	Grosvenor Aviation Services
Guernsey	HW	GER	Guernsey Airlines Ltd
Guest Keen	KN	GKN	GKN Group Services Ltd
Gulf Air	GF	GFA	Gulf Air
Hamlin	—	HAV	Hamlin Aviation Ltd
Hatair	—	—	Hatfield Executive Aviation Ltd
Hawker	—	DUN	Dunsfold BAe
Hubbardair	—	HBD	Hubbardair Ltd
Hunting	—	—	Hunting Surveys Ltd
Hyde	—	—	Hyde VIP Helicopters
Iberia	IB	IBE	Iberia
Iceair	FI	ICE	Icelandair
Interflight	—	IFT	Interflight Ltd
Japanair	JL	JAL	Japan Airlines
Jersey	JY	JEA	Jersey European Airways
Jetplan	—	JPN	Memrykord Ltd
Jolly	—	—	USAF HH-53 rescue helicopters
Kentair	—	—	Surrey and Kent Flying Club Ltd
Kilro	—	AKL	Air Kilroe

R/T callsign	2-letter code	3-letter code	Operation
King	—	—	67th Aerospace Rescue Squadron USAF (C-130)
Kitty	—	—	Queen's Flight (Positioning and training Flights)
Kittyhawk	—	—	Queen's Flight (HM Queen on board) or certain other members of Royal Family.)
KLM	KL	KLM	KLM-Royal Dutch Airlines
Kondair	—	KND	Kondair Ltd
Koreanair	KE	KAL	Korean Airlines
Lark	—	—	55th Weather Recce Squadron USAF (C-130)
Lauda	LW	LDA	Lauda-Air
Leck	—	LEC	Lec Refrigeration
Leopard	—	—	Queen's Flight (Prince Andrew on board)
Lion	—	BIH	British International Helicopters
Logan	LC	LOG	Loganair Ltd
Lord	—	—	207th Aviation Company US Army Heidelberg
Losalt	—	KCL	Jubilee Airways Ltd
Lot (Pollot)	LO	LOT	Lot, Poland
Lovo	—	LVO	Lovaux Ltd
Luxair	LG	LGL	Luxair
MAC	—	—	Military Airlift Command, USAF
MacDonald	—	—	McDonald Aviation Ltd
Macline	RM	MCH	McAlpine Aviation Ltd
Malinair	—	MAK	Malinair
Mamair	MF	MMM	MAM Aviation Ltd
Mann	—	AMH	Alan Mann Helicopters Ltd
Manx	—	MNX	Manx Airlines Ltd
March	—	MAR	March Helicopters Ltd
Marshall	—	MCE	Marshall of Cambridge (Engineering) Ltd
Martin	—	MBE	Martin-Baker Ltd
Martinair	MP	MPH	Martinair Holland
Midas	—	MDS	Mildford Docks Air Service Ltd
Midland	BD	BMA	British Midland Airways Ltd
Minair	MC	CFU	CAA Flying Unit
Merlin	—	RRL	Rolls Royce (Military Aviation)
Metman	—	MRF	Meteorological Research Flight
Metpol	—	—	Metropolitan Police Flying Club
Monarch	OM	MON	Monarch Airlines Ltd
Moth	—	—	Tiger Fly
Myson	—	—	Myson Group
National	MO	MAA	Airmore Aviation

R/T callsign	2-letter code	3-letter code	Operation
Navy	—	NVY	Royal Navy
Navy	—	—	US Navy
Neatax	NV	NEX	Northern Executive Aviation Ltd
Newpin	—	NEW	Hawarden BAe
Nightflight	—	NFG	Night Flight Ltd
Nordic	—	NDC	Nordic Air Services
Northair	NT	NTL	Northern Air Taxis Ltd
November Papa	NP	HLA	Heavylift Cargo Airlines Ltd
Nugget	—	RAE	Farnborough RAE
Olympic	OA	OAL	Olympic Airways
Optica	—	OPT	Edgley Aircraft Ltd
Orange	HD	AHD	Air Holland
Optica	—	OPT	Edgley Aircraft Ltd
Orion	KG	ORN	Orion Airways Ltd
Orkney	—	ORK	Air Orkney
Para	—	—	Army Parachute Centre
Peacock	—	PCK	Peacock H E & Sons (Thorney) Ltd
Pearl	OJ	OJA	Oriental Pearl Airways Ltd
Peregrine	PJ	PSS	Peregrine Air Services Ltd
People	—	—	People Express
Plum	—	PLM	PLM Helicopters
Puma	—	PLP	Phoenix Aviation
Quantas	QF	QFA	Quantas Airways
Rafair	—	RFR	Royal Air Force
Rainbow	—	—	Queen's Flight (HRH Prince Philip on board)
Rankjet	—	—	Rank Organisation Ltd
Rapeed	—	—	Southern Joyrides Ltd
Rogav	—	RAV	Rogers Aviation Ltd
Rolls	BT	BTU	Rolls Royce Ltd (Bristol Engine Div)
Roycar	—	—	Rolls Royce Ltd
Rushton	—	FLR	Flight Refuelling Ltd
Ryanair	—	RYR	Ryanair
Ryburn	—	—	Ryburn Air Ltd
Sabena	SN	SAB	Sabena, Belgian World Airlines
SAM	—	—	Special Air Mission (USAF)
Sarnair	GD	GJD	Channel Aviation Ltd
Saudi	SV	SVA	Saudi-Arabian Airlines
Scandinavian	SK	SAS	Scandinavian Airlines System
Scottish Express	—	SEI	Scottish Express International
Servisair	MJ	SGH	Servisair Ltd
Shamrock	EI	EIN	Aer Lingus
Shell	—	SHE	Shell Aircraft Ltd

R/T callsign	2-letter code	3-letter code	Operation
Short	—	SBL	Short Brothers Ltd
Shuttle	BA	—	British Airways (certain internal flights)
Simflight	—	SIM	Simulated Flight Training Ltd
Singapore	SQ	SIA	Singapore Airlines
Skybird	—	—	Anywair Travel (UK) Ltd
Skyfame	—	—	Skyfame Ltd
Skyguard	—	SKD	Skyguard Ltd
Skyship	—	AIS	Skyship Industries UK Ltd
Sloane	—	SLN	Sloane Aviation
Southendair	—	—	SPT Aircraft Ltd
Spar	—	—	58th Military Airlift Squadron Rhein-Mein
Speedbird	BA	BAW	British Airways
Spooner	—	—	Spooner Aviation Ltd
Springbok	—	SAA	South African Airways
Sterling	NB	SAW	Sterling Airways
Swissair	SR	SWR	Swissair
Tarnish	—	WTN	Warton BAe
Tarom	RO	ROT	Tarom Romanian Air Transport
Tarnish	—	WTN	Warton BAe
Tennant	—	PWK	Prestwick BAe
Tester	—	TPS	Empire Test Pilots School, Boscombe Down
Thai Inter	TH	TAC	Thai International
Thurston	HZ	THG	Thurston Aviation Ltd
Tibbet	—	HFD	Hatfield BAe
Tiger	FT	FTL	Flying Tiger
Tradewinds	IK	IKA	Tradewinds Airways Ltd
Transamerica	TV	TVA	Transamerica Airlines
Trans Europe	—	TEU	Trans Europe Air Charter Ltd
Trehaven	JF	PMF	Crest Aviation
Turkair	TK	THY	Turkish Airlines
Ukay	UK	UKA	Air UK Ltd
Unicorn	—	—	Queen's Flight (HRH Prince Charles on board)
UTA	UT	UTA	UTA (France)
Varig	RG	VRG	Varig Brazil
Vectis	—	PBN	Pilatus Britten Norman Ltd
Veritair	—	VRT	Veritair Ltd
Vickers	—	VSB	Vickers Ship Building Group
Viking	DK	VKG	Scanair Ltd
Virgin	—	VIR	Virgin Atlantic
Wardair	WD	WDA	Wardair Canada
Watchdog	—	FPA	Ministry of Agriculture, Fisheries and Food
Welshair	—	CYM	Airways International Cymru Ltd

R/T callsign	2-letter code	3-letter code	Operation
Westland	—	WHE	Westland Helicopters Ltd
West London	—	WLA	West London Aero Services Ltd
Wigwam	NR	CSE	CSE Aviation Ltd
Woodair	—	WOD	Woodgate Air Services
World	WO	WOA	World Airways
Yoobee	—	—	United Biscuit Co Ltd
Yorkair	—	—	Yorkshire Flying Services Ltd

Suffixes to the flight number have various meanings:

A Extra flight on the same route. If more than one B, C etc may be used

F Freight

P Positioning flight

Q Aircraft operating on a repetitive flight plan where some fundamental detail has been changed for the particular flight, for example the aircraft type

R Freight. Appears to be unique to Lufthansa.

T Training flight

X Allocated by ATC when two aircraft from different companies but with the same flight number are on the same frequency and there is a likelihood of confusion.

Note that British Airways Shuttle callsigns, for example Shuttle 6Z, are unique to this operation.

Britannia Airways has its own system in which the suffixes A and B signify outbound and inboard flights, eg

BY220A Luton to Milan

BY220B Milan to Luton

Index